STUDY GUIDE

UNDERSTANDING MANAGEMENT

SECOND EDITION

RICHARD L. DAFT
Vanderbilt University

DOROTHY MARCIC
University of Economics—Prague

HAROLD C. BABSON
Columbus State Community College

MURRAY S. BRUNTON
Central Ohio Technical College

The Dryden Press
Harcourt Brace College Publishers
Fort Worth Philadelphia San Diego New York Orlando Austin San Antonio
Toronto Montreal London Sydney Tokyo

Address for Editorial Correspondence:
Harcourt Brace College Publishers, 301 Commerce Street, Suite 3700, Fort Worth, TX 76102

Address for Orders:
Harcourt Brace & Company, 6277 Sea Harbor Drive, Orlando, FL 32887-6777
1-800-782-4479, or 1-800-433-0001 (in Florida)

ISBN: 0-03-024737-3

Printed in the United States of America

" 7 8 9 0 1 2 3 4 5 6 202 9 8 7 6 5 4 3 2 "

The Dryden Press
Harcourt Brace & Company

PREFACE

This *Study Guide* has been developed to accompany the second edition of *Understanding Management* by Daft and Marcic. The two primary goals of the guide are to allow students to enhance their learning of the basic concepts covered in the text and, in turn, help them apply those concepts to a variety of situations.

We strongly believe that the combination of enhanced learning and skill development will better prepare students to compete in the ever-changing world of management.

Each chapter in the *Study Guide* corresponds to a chapter in the text and consists of the following:

Chapter Outline with Learning Objectives

Major Concepts
Summarizes major concepts presented in text.

Key Term Identification/Application
Presents a set of objective questions that help students identify key terms and apply concepts to specific situations.

- Matching Questions
- Multiple-Choice Questions

Skill Practice Exercises
Allow students to apply critical and creative problem-solving skills to a variety of scenarios, real-life experiences, and a case history.

- Just-Suppose Scenarios
- Personal Learning Experience
- Integrated Case
- Journal Entries

We urge conscientious and consistent use of the materials in this *Study Guide* with the hope that such effort will aid students in developing self-confidence in their ability to apply the basic principles of management to their personal and professional lives.

Acknowledgments

We would like to thank the following people for their invaluable contributions to this *Study Guide*:

John Bowen, Adjunct Instructor, Columbus State Community College, for his work on the chapter introductions and integrated case.

Linda Reid, for her organizational skills and good humor during the production of the *Study Guide*.

Harold C. Babson
Murray S. Brunton

CONTENTS

CHAPTER 1—THE CHANGING PARADIGM OF MANAGEMENT

Chapter Outline	Corresponding Learning Objectives
I. The Definition of Management	L.O. 1 Explain the management revolution and how it will affect you as a future manager.
II. The Four Management Functions ● Planning ● Organizing ● Leading ● Controlling	L.O. 2 Describe the four management functions and the type of management activity associated with each.
III. Organizational Performance	L.O. 3 Explain the difference between efficiency and effectiveness and their importance for organizational performance.
IV. Management Skills ● Conceptual Skills ● Human Skills ● Technical Skills	L.O. 4 Describe conceptual, human, and technical skills and their relevance for managers and nonmanagers.
V. Management Types ● Vertical Differences ● Horizontal Differences	L.O. 5 Define functional, general, and project managers.
VI. What Is It Like to Be a Manager? ● Manager Activities ● Manager Roles	L.O. 6 Define ten roles that managers perform in organizations.
VII. Managing in Small Businesses and Not-for-Profit Organizations	
VIII. Leading the Management Revolution ● Preparing for the Year 2000 ● The Learning Organization	L.O. 7 Describe the learning organization and the issues managers must prepare for in the future.

Major Concepts

(1) Managers are assigned the responsibility of efficiently using their organization's resources in order to effectively achieve its goals. (2) To fulfill that responsibility, they play informational, interpersonal, and decisional roles and employ conceptual, human, and technical skills as they perform the basic management functions of planning, organizing, leading, and controlling.   (3) If there is more than one manager, each one may be organized into a vertical hierarchy with certain horizontal managers specializing in specific functions such as marketing, human resources, operations, and finance; some managers with responsibilities that are more general (involving more than one function); and others who move from project to project.   (4) Regardless of whether the organizations they manage are large or small, profit or not-for-profit, the managers increasingly require fundamental changes in mind-sets, management of patterns rather than day-to-day events, use of diversity, global orientation, and reinvention into learning organizations.

In your own words, *what did the above paragraph say*? Can you give some examples using current business news or your own experiences? Perhaps the following will help you translate the above and strengthen your understanding of the first chapter!

First Sentence: Using Resources to Achieve Goals
A for-profit organization such as GE or IBM may not have the same goals as a not-for-profit organization such as a church or military organization. Nevertheless, managers use human, financial, and other resources to achieve their goals.   If they actually achieve their goals, they are effective.   If they achieve those goals using as few resources as possible, they are efficient. Managers seek to be both effective and efficient.

Second Sentence: Roles, Skills, and Basic Management Functions
Roles: informational roles such as monitor, disseminator, and spokesperson help maintain and develop an information network; interpersonal roles such as figurehead, leader, and liaison involve relationships with others; and decisional roles such as entrepreneur, disturbance handler, resource allocator, and negotiator involve requirements for the manager to choose and take action. In other words, the manager's informational roles involve managing communication, the interpersonal roles involve managing humans, and the decisional roles involve making something happen.

Skills: conceptual skills involve thinking, information processing, and planning ability; human skills involve the ability to work with and through other people and groups; and technical skills involve understanding and mastery of tasks, methods, techniques, and equipment. In essence, the manager must be able to use his or her mind (conceptual skills), other people (human skills), and specific activities or tools (technical skills).

Conceptual skills are most important for the CEO, technical skills are most important for the first-line supervisor, and human skills are important for all.

Basic Management Functions: the basic management functions consist of planning, organizing, leading, and controlling.   They are comparable to what you must do in order to take a trip.   You plan by determining where you are going and the route you will use to get there, you organize by determining who is going to drive and who will read the map, you lead by developing enthusiasm on the part of all who will have a role in the trip, and you establish controls by watching the highway signs to be sure that you are moving toward your destination. Managers plan: they need to set goals and select the best means of achieving those goals. They organize the work that must be done and the human and financial resources required in order to accomplish the plan.   They lead by sharing their vision of the goals they are planning to achieve, and they develop support for all that will be required for success. They establish controls to be sure the resources are being used effectively and efficiently as the organization moves toward its goals.

Third Sentence: Vertical/Horizontal; General, Functional, and Project Managers

These concepts are interrelated. The chain of command from the CEO to the first-level supervisor is the vertical structure, but when one views any given level (the horizontal view) one may note that some managers on the same level may be functional managers: they specialize in only one function such as operations, human resources, finance, or marketing. Other managers at that level may be general managers: they may have responsibility for more than one of these functions.   Since the CEO has responsibility for all functional areas of the organization, the CEO is always a general manager. Project managers are similar to general managers in that they must understand the various functional areas of an organization, but they are different in the sense that they play a coordinative role focusing on a particular need that may arise such as new product development.

Fourth Sentence: Organizational Size, Purpose, and Change

Regardless of the organization's size (large or small) or purpose (profit or not-for-profit), managers need to manage change if they and their organization are to survive and succeed. Current large size and profitability does not ensure survival: during the past decade major corporations have become unprofitable and disappeared or have been overtaken by what were once small ventures. Being involved in a worthy not-for-profit purpose does not ensure the organization that it will continue to be funded. Survival and success in the Year 2000 and beyond require revolutionary management. This involves so-called paradigm shifts or changes in mind-sets, management of patterns based on "chaos theory"—the recognition that often day-to-day events are random and unpredictable; use of diversity in the work force as an asset; global orientation as national boundaries become less significant in the movement of money, people, and goods; and reinvention into learning organizations that constantly adapt to new realities and expand capabilities.

Key Term Identification/Application

Matching Questions

Match each statement or situation with the key term that best describes it.

a.	management	k.	middle manager
b.	role	l.	functional manager
c.	organizing	m.	effectiveness
d.	first-line manager	n.	human skill
e.	leading	o.	top manager
f.	organization	p.	general manager
g.	planning	q.	technical skill
h.	conceptual skill	r.	performance
i.	controlling	s.	paradigm
j.	efficiency	t.	project manager

_____ 1.   Assigning tasks, grouping tasks into departments, and allocating resources to departments.

_____ 2.   The degree to which the organization achieves a stated goal.

_____ 3.   The attainment of organizational goals in an effective and efficient manner through planning, organizing, leading, and controlling organizational resources.

_____ 4.   The organization's ability to attain its goals in an effective and efficient manner.

_____ 5.   The use of influence to motivate employees to achieve organizational goals.

_____ 6.   Using minimal resources to produce a desired volume of output.

_____ 7.   Defining goals for future organizational performance and deciding on the tasks and resources needed to attain them.

_____ 8.   A social entity that is goal directed and deliberately structured.

_____ 9.   Monitoring employees' activities, determining whether the organization is on target toward its goals, and making corrections as needed.

_____ 10.   A manager who is responsible for the entire organization and who is at the top of the organizational hierarchy.

_____ 11.   The understanding of, and proficiency in, the performance of specific tasks.

_____ 12.   A set of expectations for one's behavior.

_____ 13.   The ability to see the organization as a whole and the relationship among its parts.

_____ 14.   One who is responsible for a temporary work project that involves the participation of other people at a similar level in the organization.

_____ 15.   One who works at the middle levels of the organization and is responsible for major departments.

_____ 16.   The ability to work with and through other people and to work effectively as a group member.

_____ 17.   One who is directly responsible for the production of goods and services and who is at the first or second management level.

_____ 18.   One who is responsible for several departments that perform different functions.

_____ 19.   A mind-set that presents a fundamental way of thinking, perceiving, and understanding the world.

_____ 20.   One who is responsible for a department that performs a single functional task and has employees with similar training and skills.

Multiple-Choice Questions

Consider the following situations and, utilizing the appropriate management concepts, answer the multiple-choice questions that follow.

Situation #1

You have recently been hired as a manager-in-training in the new fast-food chain Brats-R-Us. One of your initial tasks is working at all the various work stations in the restaurant. You are also responsible for coordinating the scheduling of the many part-time workers the store employs.

1. By assigning you to work three days at every work station, it is clear that the Brats-R-Us training program is initially designed to develop your:

    a.   technical skills.
    b.   conceptual skills.
    c.   organizational skills.
    d.   human skills.

2. After your three-day work station rotation, you are assigned to run the 3:00 pm–closing shift. You are directly responsible for the employees' performance on your shift, so you are very concerned with how to lead and motivate them. In terms of management level you are a:

    a.   top manager.
    b.   middle manager.
    c.   first-line manager.
    d.   none of the above.

3. Your store manager has communicated to you the importance of controlling costs because of the slim profit margin under which the store is operating. It is evident that the store manager is VERY concerned with:

    a.   effectiveness.
    b.   efficiency.
    c.   leading.
    d.   organizing.

4.   The store manager also stresses the importance of reaching the sales quotas, or goals, that the district manager has assigned. This achievement of the sales goal indicates a strong emphasis on:

      a.   planning.
      b.   technical skills.
      c.   efficiency.
      d.   effectiveness.

5.   You are slowly starting to realize the joint and equal importance of reaching organizational goals in an effective and efficient manner, which is called organizational:

      a.   leading.
      b.   performance.
      c.   paradigms.
      d.   controlling.

Situation #2

For several weeks now you have run your shift in an effective and efficient manner. The store manager has decided to challenge you with the task of scheduling all shifts for the entire restaurant.

6.   As you spend your time ensuring that you are scheduling enough employees for the appropriate times and days, you are aware that you are deeply involved in the managerial function of:

      a.   planning.
      b.   leading.
      c.   organizing.
      d.   controlling.

7.   You have a weekly target of 21.6% labor cost, which is a measurement of the relationship between sales and labor dollars spent. After the weekly figures are compiled and compared against the standard, you know that you will be rewarded for meeting the standard and penalized for exceeding the standard. This is evidence of the managerial function of:

      a.   planning.
      b.   leading.
      c.   organizing.
      d.   controlling.

8.   It seems that much of your time in the store is spent on the floor with employees attempting to motivate them to achieve the organizational goals. These efforts fall under the managerial function of:

    a.   planning.
    b.   leading.
    c.   organizing.
    d.   controlling.

9.   Next week all the managers in the district will be meeting to establish the goals for the district for the new year and also determining what has to be done and what resources are needed in order to accomplish the goals. This is a good example of the managerial function of:

    a.   planning.
    b.   leading.
    c.   organizing.
    d.   controlling.

10.   In order to do a good job at the district meeting (which will focus on goal setting and determining how to achieve those goals), it is essential that every manager possess good:

    a.   human skills.
    b.   conceptual skills.
    c.   technical skills.
    d.   performing skills.

Situation #3

Over the past five years you have been promoted from manager-in-training to first-shift manager, to dining room manager, and finally to manager of your own unit. Congratulations!

11.   As the dining room manager, you were responsible for the performance of that department and all the employees in that department. You were a(an):

    a.   operational manager.
    b.   general manager.
    c.   functional manager.
    d.   middle manager.

12.   As the manager of your own unit, you have total operational responsibility for all the departments and personnel in your unit. You are a(an):

   a.   middle manager.
   b.   general manager.
   c.   first-line manager.
   d.   functional manager.

13.   Last week the district manager paid you a big compliment by appointing you in charge of the team that will investigate and recommend whether or not the district should change some of its operational policies. The other members of the team are also unit managers. You are operating as a(an):

   a.   functional manager.
   b.   top manager.
   c.   general manager.
   d.   project manager.

14.   As a general manager, you are expected, at times, to perform different behaviors such as negotiator, spokesperson, resource allocator, and disturbance handler. These various expectations of your behavior amount to:

   a.   roles.
   b.   parts.
   c.   plays.
   d.   acts.

15.   One of the very important lessons that you have learned over time is that things are constantly changing. With this change sometimes comes the necessity of changing your way of thinking about, perceiving, and understanding your business and your industry. Your mind-set about your business and your industry is a(an):

   a.   example of chaos theory.
   b.   paradigm.
   c.   role.
   d.   conceptual skill.

Skill Practice Exercises

Just-Suppose Scenarios

Scenario #1

Just suppose that upon graduation you are hired as a management trainee at an internationally known women's retail clothing chain. Your responsibilities will include, but are not limited to, supervising and scheduling of employees and inventory control. As you face this challenge, you try to recall some important concepts from your college days concerning the nature of management.

1.   Describe your position in terms of level of management and type of management.

2.   Describe in detail how the four functions of management apply to you and your position.

3.   Identify the three types of management skills. Now evaluate yourself in terms of those skills. Which of those skills do you need to improve the most?

Scenario #2

Just suppose that a few years have passed. You are now the unit manager of one of the higher volume stores in the chain, and you have full responsibility for its operation.

1.   Describe and explain how your management level has changed, how your responsibilities have changed, and how the four functions of management now apply to you.

2.   Yesterday you noticed two of your sales associates engaged in a ten-minute gossip session while ignoring the customers in the store. Discuss this in terms of effectiveness, efficiency, and performance.

3.   It is very important to you that you be a successful manager. How do you define success? How do you plan to accomplish this?

Scenario #3

After five years at the unit manager level, you have been promoted to district manager, with your district encompassing thirty stores. You have decided to have a district meeting of all thirty unit managers.

1.   As you prepare for the meeting, reflect upon what the four functions of management mean to you now.

2.   Which management concepts remain uppermost in your mind as you approach this meeting?

3.   What does the concept of paradigm mean to you at this point in time?

Personal Learning Experience

Interview

Contact a local business with which you are familiar, such as a restaurant, video store, or grocery store. Make an appointment to talk with the manager. At the meeting discuss the following:

A.   How long has this person been the manager? What, if any, changes has this person seen or experienced in terms of the employees, the customers, and the suppliers of the business?

B.   What are the major challenges facing this manager? How does this manager plan to cope or deal with these challenges?

C.   Describe a "normal day" for this manager. What level is this manager? What types of roles does this manager perform?

Integrated Case

LDX TechnoSystems

LDX TechnoSystems is primarily involved in providing hi-tech training. It was once part of AmCom Limited, a major telecommunications corporation, but AmCom wanted to focus its efforts on only a very limited line of services, so it chose to get rid of its training activities. LDX executives pooled their money, bought LDX, and now had a corporation free to pursue whatever opportunities it chose without being held back by AmCom. People who were previously only managers of one small part of another corporation were now top management in their own corporation.

LDX executives were excited by what this new freedom might mean. When they were part of AmCom, they had to deal with a highly structured, multilevel chain of command, which tended to slow down decision making. The more important and urgent a problem or opportunity, the higher in the chain of command the issue had to go before a decision could be made. As a result, LDX was constantly losing opportunities to more flexible, less structured organizations. Worse, the decisions involving technology were being made by people who had very little knowledge of technology—many of the higher executives at AmCom were computer illiterates. For a long time, AmCom could afford the luxury of such an approach to management because they had a patent that protected them from competition on their main product. However, LDX managers knew that once the patent expired and AmCom had to compete with more innovative, knowledgeable, lower-cost companies in the U.S. and overseas, the dinosaur AmCom would eventually become extinct. Severing LDX from AmCom provided an opportunity to jump a sinking ship. LDX could now become the same type of vigorous and thriving organization as any of the competitors. However, changing LDX proved to be a monumental challenge that took several years to accomplish.

One of the first challenges was to answer the following: "What is LDX? What are we trying to accomplish and who are we trying to do it for?" AmCom used to answer questions such as that. LDX existed primarily to provide whatever training was needed by the various divisions of AmCom. Those divisions were required to use LDX's services even if there were less expensive or better services available from competitors. Now that LDX was free of AmCom, AmCom was also free of LDX—and might likely use LDX's competitors. Another challenge involved their human resources and their various assets. LDX resources were selected to meet AmCom needs and were often obtained from other divisions of AmCom at inflated costs. Many of the people at LDX actually came from AmCom, spending most of their careers in other areas of the corporation and then transferring to LDX for their few remaining years until retirement.

The executives who bought out AmCom selected from among themselves the people who would serve on their board of directors, including their Chief Executive Officer (CEO), Al Roberts. Al had always served in Finance, and it was his financial expertise that had helped them buy LDX from AmCom. Al now needed to figure out how he was going to deal with the LDX management challenges.

Case Questions

1.   Based on the limited information available, compare AmCom and LDX management. Which is most likely to be efficient? Which is most likely to be effective?

2.   Which of the management functions would appear to be most important to LDX at this time?   Why?   Which is the second most important?   Why?

3.   Which of the management skills would appear to be most important to Al Roberts at this time?   Why?   Which is the second most important?   Why?

4.   Which of the management roles would appear to be most important to Al Roberts at this time?   Why?   Which is the second most important? Why?

5.   What paradigm shifts are needed in LDX management to prepare for the future?   Discuss whether Al Roberts's management background would help or hinder such a shift as opposed to a person with a general management background.

Journal Entries

Directions

The student Study Guide will include a requirement that you keep a journal of your thoughts from class discussions and corresponding chapter assignments as described below.

For class discussions and each chapter covered, you will log the following journal entries:

1.   A summary description of Chapter 1 class discussions.

2.   A brief description of one <u>personal</u> <u>management</u> <u>activity</u> relating to class discussion in Chapter 1. The activity could include the planning for a committee meeting at church or leading a fund-raising effort for your local civic association.

3.   A brief description of one <u>managerial</u> <u>incident</u> you have encountered <u>at work</u> as it relates to class discussion in Chapter 1. This incident may include a look at your manager and how he or she demonstrates one of the skills a manager needs to get the job done; namely, conceptual, human, or technical.

4.   Reflections on the interrelationship of the class discussions and the out-of-class activity and incident you have recorded in 2 and 3.

In this way, you will be reporting on and verifying to what degree what you have read in the text and experienced in the classroom matches the reality of your daily personal and business life.

Your goals will be to better understand how managers really get things done through planning, organizing, leading, and controlling resources and by interacting with the firm's outside environment.

Also, this journal will serve as a means of developing your own critical thinking ability as well as your writing skill.

1.   Summary of Class Discussion

_____

_____

_____

_____

_____

_____

_____

_____

_____

_____

_____

_____

_____

_____

2.   Personal Management Activity

Activity 1 _____

_____

_____

_____

Description 1 _____

_____

_____

_____

3.   Managerial Incident Encountered

Incident 1 _____

_____

_____

_____

Description 1 _____

_____

_____

_____

4.   Reflections on Class Discussion as Related to:

Activity 1 _____

_____

_____

_____

_____

_____

_____

_____

Incident 1 _____

_____

_____

_____

_____

_____

_____

Chapter 1 Answer Key

Matching

Question	Answer	Question	Answer
1	c	11	q
2	m	12	b
3	a	13	h
4	r	14	t
5	e	15	k
6	j	16	n
7	g	17	d
8	f	18	p
9	i	19	s
10	o	20	l

Multiple Choice

Question	Answer	Question	Answer
1	a	9	a
2	c	10	b
3	b	11	c
4	d	12	b
5	b	13	d
6	c	14	a
7	d	15	b
8	b		

CHAPTER 2—FOUNDATIONS OF LEARNING ORGANIZATIONS

Chapter Outline	Corresponding Learning Objectives
I. The Revolution in Management • Chaotic Environment • Paradigm Shift	L.O. 1 Discuss the causes of the current revolution in management thinking.
II. The Learning Organization • The Learning Manager • The Learning Organization • Leadership • Horizontal Structure • Employee Empowerment • Communication/Information Sharing • Emergent Strategy • Strong Culture	L.O. 2 Describe the concept of the learning organization as it relates to managers and to organizations. L.O. 3 Discuss how a learning organization is designed through changes in leadership, structure, empowerment, information, sharing, strategy, and culture.
III. Historical Forces Leading Up to the Learning Organization	L.O. 4 Understand how historical forces in society have influenced the practice of management.
IV. Classical Perspective • Scientific Management • Bureaucratic Organizations • Administrative Principles	L.O. 5 Identify and explain major developments in the history of management thought.
V. Humanistic Perspective • The Human Relations Movement • The Human Resources Perspective • The Behavioral Sciences Approach	L.O. 6 Describe the major components of the classical management perspective.
VI. Management Science Perspective	L.O. 7 Describe the major compoenents of the humanistic management perspective. L.O. 8 Discuss the quantitative management perspective.

Chapter Outline	Corresponding Learning Objectives

VII. Contemporary Extensions
  • Systems Theory
  • Contingency View
 	
VIII. Recent Historical Trends
  • Globalization
  • Total Quality Management
	L.O. 9 Discuss the basic concepts of systems theory.
	
	L.O. 10 Describe the recent influences of global competition on management in North America.

Major Concepts

(1) The paradigm shift of management focus from stability to problem solving and change has resulted in new organizational structures and relationships as epitomized by the learning organization. (2) The current management revolution is a continuation of past classical, humanistic, and management science perspectives and is affected by contemporary systems theory and contingency views. (3) Recent trends toward globalization and total quality management affect each other and the overall management revolution.

In your own words, *what did the above paragraph say?*   Perhaps the following will help you translate the above and strengthen your understanding of the second chapter!

First Sentence: The Paradigm Shift's Results and the Learning Organization

A paradigm shift is a fundamental change in thinking; changes in technology, the external environment, and global competition have produced changes in organizational management so as to manage such changes. In particular, managers must be problem solvers and be part of an organizational structure that can better respond to change than the traditional vertical hierarchy with its top-down controls. The horizontal relationships in empowered teams tend to be better able to thrive under continuous change than such traditional vertical relationships.   The epitome of horizontal relationships (which can respond to volatile change) is the learning organization: an organization with visionary leaders, strong culture, empowered employees and shared information.

Second Sentence: The Current Revolution — A Result of the Past and the Contemporary

The end of the old social contract of assured employment and the recent downsizing suggest—that a management revolution is now occurring.

In the past, the perspectives that enabled managers to improve productivity included three perspectives: (1) classical, (2) humanistic, and (3) management science.

First, let's look at the classical perspective. It focused on "working smarter" through three approaches: the approach of scientific management, which involved a systematic analysis of work and how it was managed, the bureaucracy approach, and the approach involving the guidance of administrative principles. Examples of the use of these perspectives would include scientific management's attempt to find the one best way to do things, bureaucratic attempts to ensure fairness and continuity in how things are done, and administrative principles that can guide the entire organization regarding the elements of management and how those elements should function.

Second, let's look at the humanistic perspective. It recognized that in order for managers to be truly productive in getting things done through people, they need to better understand their employees and other people in the organization. The human relations movement was helped by the Hawthorne experiments, which were originally undertaken as an example of scientific management and were directed to issues such as effective lighting.

The improved productivity obtained during the experiments appeared to be due more to the attention being given to workers than any changes in lighting. As a result, organizations began to focus not just on the management of production but on the management of the human resources used in the production. Departments were established for that sole purpose.

In contrast to scientific management, which carefully studied work and how it was managed, the behavioral science perspective used scientific methods to study people and thereby understand their behavior and interactions within organizations.

The third perspective, scientific management, focused on tools to help mangers make better decisions as they manage the work and the workers. The tools include math, statistics, and management information systems—sometimes simply called "MIS"—which is the use of computers to facilitate decisions.

The above three perspectives continue to be useful today. One of the perspectives, the humanistic, has evolved into two contemporary extensions: systems theory and the contingency view. Systems theory examines how the interrelated parts and subsystems function together to achieve synergy. This synergy defines the common purpose as being better achieved working together than individually and without entropy (decay) as those systems interact with the external environment. The contingency view suggests that what works best in one situation may not work best in all and that managers need to adapt their approach to specific situations or cases.

Third Sentence: Effects of Globalization and Total Quality Management

In the past, managers used classical, humanistic, and management science perspectives to determine the best way to make decisions as to how they manage work and the people who do the work. We have just reviewed the modifying impact of two contemporary extensions of the past: systems theory and contingency views.

However, globalization and total quality management are two forces that are currently interacting to accelerate the current management revolution. The globalization of business means that even managers who might have little interest in business outside the U.S. are going to be affected by it and must therefore be striving to maintain the quality that can enable them to not only survive against domestic competitors but potential overseas competitors as well. Unlike in the past, when managers sought the one best way, survival against all the potential competitors on planet earth places more pressure on managers to implement a key aim of total quality management—to strive for continuous improvement.

Instead of resting when one achieves some given quality advantage that can enable the firm to survive against current known threats, the organization strives for ever higher quality to give it an advantage in moving ahead of others around the world.

Key Term Identification/Application

Matching Questions

Match each statement or situation with the key term that best describes it. (Note: Some terms will not be used.)

a.	paradigm	n.	behavioral sciences approach
b.	learning organization	o.	management science perspective
c.	social forces		
d.	political forces	p.	system
e.	economic forces	q.	systems theory
f.	classical perspective	r.	open system
g.	scientific management	s.	closed system
h.	bureaucratic organizations	t.	entropy
i.	administrative principles	u.	synergy
j.	humanistic perspective	v.	subsystems
k.	Hawthorne studies	w.	contingency view
l.	human relations movement	x.	Theory Z
m.	human resources perspective	y.	total quality management (TQM)

_____ 1.   The management perspective that emerged after World War II and applied mathematics, statistics, and other quantitative techniques to managerial problems.

_____ 2.   The tendency for a system to run down and die.

_____ 3.   An organization in which everyone is engaged in identifying and solving problems.

_____ 4.   An early twentieth century management perspective that emphasized a rational, scientific approach to the study of management in order to make organizations efficient operating machines.

_____ 5.   Managing the total organization to deliver quality to customers through employee involvement, focus on the customer, benchmarking, and continuous improvement.

_____ 6.   A late nineteenth century management perspective that emphasized the understandingof human behavior, needs, and attitudes in the workplace.

_____ 7.   Parts of a system that depend upon each other for their functioning.

_____ 8.   A management perspective that maintains that jobs should be designed to meet higher-level needs by allowing workers to use their full potential.

_____ 9.   The whole is greater than the sum of its parts.

_____ 10.   The influence of political and legal institutions on people and organizations.

_____ 11.   The subfield of classical management that proposed management on an impersonal and rational basis, utilizing concepts such as clearly defined authority and responsibility.

_____ 12.   A set of interrelated parts that functions as a whole in order to achieve a common purpose.

_____ 13.   A movement in management thinking that emphasized satisfaction of employees' basic needs as the key to increased worker productivity.

_____ 14.   A system that interacts with the external environment.

_____ 15.   A fundamental way of thinking about, perceiving, and understanding the world.

_____ 16.   A management perspective that combines techniques from both Japanese and North American management practices.

_____ 17.   The successful resolution of organizational problems depends on managers' identification of key variables in the situation.

_____ 18.   A system that does not interact with the external environment.

_____ 19.   The aspects of a culture that guide and influence relationships among people—such as values and standards of behavior.

_____ 20.   The subfield of classical management that focused upon the total organization rather than the individual worker and established the management functions of planning, organizing, controlling, and coordinating.

Multiple-Choice Questions

Consider the following situations and, utilizing the appropriate management concepts, answer the multiple-choice questions that follow.

Situation #1

In order to get a better grasp of the concepts presented in class concerning a learning organization and the principles of management, you have decided to take a tour of the campus and talk to several students, faculty, and staff.

1.   One of the things that becomes instantly apparent concerning the students is that they are so varied and diverse. There are many young students, but there are also a great number of nontraditional students returning to the educational environment. Apparently there has been a shift in the educational:

      a.   administrative principles.
      b.   economic forces.
      c.   paradigm.
      d.   political forces.

2.   After talking with several members of the college's administrative staff, it has become apparent to you that they are very concerned about the drop in enrollment over the last three or four years. At least part of that can be accounted for by the steady growth of the economy, or:

      a.   political forces.
      b.   economic forces.
      c.   social forces.
      d.   none of the above.

3.   As you turn the corner of a building, you notice several students huddled together, bracing themselves against the wind while they smoke their cigarettes. This scene is evidence of the changes brought about by:

      a.   social forces.
      b.   economic forces.
      c.   political forces.
      d.   none of the above.

4. As you glance through the college bulletin from a management point of view, you are surprised by the amount of rules and procedures that are evident at the school. It is clear that various functions of the college are impersonal, and there are clear lines of authority and responsibility in each. At least from this point of view, the college is a(an):

a. learning organization.
b. entropic system.
c. scientific organization.
d. bureaucratic organization.

5. After examining the posted job vacancies and meeting with the Human Resource Director, it is clear to you that the college approach to staffing is matching the person with a job, where various elements have been clearly identified and created into a specialty. This approach to staffing can be traced to:

a. the human resource perspective.
b. scientific management.
c. human relations perspective.
d. humanistic perspective.

6. Despite this highly rational and impersonal view of jobs, employees, and the organization as a whole, some of the managers have told you that they believe in managing their subordinates in a way that indicates that they trust the employees and that the employees will accept responsibility if it is given to them. These assumptions are the foundation of:

a. Theory Z.
b. Theory X.
c. Theory Y.
d. Theory A.

7. Although you are relieved to discover that individual managers can treat their subordinates with respect and believe that most employees do not need extensive layers of rules and procedures, you feel that jobs should be designed in such a way as to allow the employees to reach their full potential at work. You are an advocate of the:

a. human resources perspective.
b. humanistic perspective.
c. classical perspective.
d. behavioral sciences perspective.

8.   When questioned about some of the school's procedures and policies, several of the faculty indicated that the administration should view the college as a set of interrelated parts that function as a whole to achieve a common purpose rather than as separate units that need many layers of rules and procedures. The faculty are proposing that the school be viewed as a(an):

a.   closed system.
b.   subsystem.
c.   system.
d.   paradigm.

9.   It is now time to register for classes for the next semester. As you stand in one of four lines, each with approximately twelve students, you wonder if the registrar has utilized mathematical formulas to determine the number of lines that should be open to optimally serve the students. This approach would be part of the:

a.   behavioral sciences approach.
b.   human relations movement.
c.   classical perspective.
d.   management science perspective.

10.   You strongly believe that the school needs to move away from placing an emphasis on the rules and procedures in order to survive and toward an environment in which it listens and responds to all of its internal and external customers. You are arguing against _____ and for

      _____.

a.   open systems, closed systems.
b.   closed systems, open systems.
c.   bureaucratic organizations, scientific management.
d.   synergy, entropy.

Situation #2

After your examination of your college, it is crystal clear to you that not all organizations are the same, that there are several different approaches to management, and that management matters! With this realization, you know that you must find the organization that is right for you.

11.   During a job fair at the college, one recruiter, when asked about which management style his company utilizes, indicated that they don't believe in any one style and that managers are encouraged to examine the situation and then utilize the approach that is most appropriate. This organization has adopted the:

   a.   classical perspective.
   b.   human resources perspective.
   c.   systems theory view.
   d.   contingency view.

12.   The recruiter went on to say that they strongly believe in the coordinative aspect of teamwork, because the whole is greater that the sum of its parts. Apparently the organization understands and embraces the concept of:

   a.   synergy.
   b.   entropy.
   c.   TQM.
   d.   closed systems.

13.   Another recruiter emphasizes not only the high job security and long-term employment at her organization but also the high degree of employee involvement and consensual decision making, which enables the workers to provide high levels of customer service.   Her organization has adopted:

   a.   Theory W.
   b.   Theory X.
   c.   Theory Y.
   d.   Theory Z.

14.   She continues by saying that they believe EVERY employee should be involved in identifying and solving problems, which enables the organization to continuously experiment, improve, and increase its capability. Apparently this organization is a(an):

      a.   paradigm.
      b.   learning organization.
      c.   bureaucratic organization.
      d.   humanistic organization.

15.   Several recruiters indicate that they have a program that utilizes extensive employee involvement, a strong and constant focus on the customer, benchmarking, and a belief in the continuous improvement of every process at the organization. These organizations are proponents of:

      a.   systems theory.
      b.   the contingency view.
      c.   total quality management.
      d.   Theory Y.

Skill Practice Exercises

Just-Suppose Scenarios

Scenario #1

Just suppose that your professor has assigned you and four fellow students the task of preparing and presenting a seminar/presentation on the growth of terrorism in the United States.

1.   Utilizing the information provided in the text, how would you (the designated leader/manager of the group) approach the task from the classical perspective?

2.   If you were to approach this task from a humanistic perspective, what would you do?

3.   If you were a Theory Y person, how would you approach the task?

Scenario #2

Just suppose that you have been hired as a district circulation manager for your local newspaper. Your district encompasses approximately 50,000 homes and apartments, and you are responsible for increasing circulation and ensuring that subscribers receive their paper on time and in good condition.

1.   From a systems theory approach, how would you handle this situation?

2.   How would you apply the concepts of total quality management to your task?

Scenario #3

Just suppose that you are the Accounting Department manager of a medium-sized trucking company. There are twenty bookkeepers who report directly to you.

1.   Describe your management style (with specific examples if you are a Theory X manager).

2.   Describe your management style if you are a Theory Y manager.

3.   Describe your management style if you believe and practice Theory Z.

Personal Learning Experience

Observation

Identify two separate and distinct environments (for example, a restaurant, a grocery store, your college, a video store).

1.   For each of the environments that you have identified/chosen, ask the manager if you could observe him/her for a few hours as a class project. How does the manager interact with his/her employees? Which management theory does this manager appear to adopt or utilize?

2.   How would you describe this manager in terms of Theory X, Theory Y, Theory Z? Identify specific behaviors that support your conclusion.

3.   Could you label this organization as a learning organization or is it a bureaucratic organization? Why?

4.   What, if any, generalizations can you draw from the above observations?

Integrated Case

From Training into Learning

LDX TechnoSystems was both a new and an old organization. It had previously served as a training organization for giant AmCom Limited, long a leader in telecommunications. However, as a result of a management buyout, it had gained its independence from AmCom. Therefore, it was a new organization. However, it still had the same people and the same mindsets that had prevailed under the old AmCom. For example, its new CEO, Jane Rand, had been head of the organization when it was only part of AmCom.

As a result, there were multiple layers of management in a very rigid vertical management hierarchy. Most management decisions had to have concurrence from higher levels. Very important decisions required Jane's concurrence. That was the way things had always been done and it had worked well. It ensured that everything was tightly controlled, for it was believed that such controls were essential to keep costs down and quality up.

Jane did attempt to experiment by doing things somewhat differently at one of LDX's locations. She permitted a greater amount of authority to be delegated down the chain of command and made some use of teams. However, one lower-level manager took advantage of that authority and committed fraud against LDX. Furthermore, some long-time managers at that facility complained that the teams had become social organizations that were wasting time and money and were simply trying to fix things that were not broken. As a result, Jane ended that experiment.

Nevertheless, she knew that LDX would need to do something different. It no longer had its former parent AmCom as a captive customer.

LDX had provided hands-on training for telecommunications equipment and had such equipment at its training centers. Its people were experts in providing training on such equipment. Unfortunately, buyers of telecommunications equipment were beginning to buy more advanced systems and very few needed to send their people to LDX centers for training on the older equipment. An obvious solution would be to buy the newer systems, have current LDX trainers learn how to use the newer equipment, and then begin training employees of the companies who were purchasing the systems. When Jane suggested that possibility to an executive committee, they unanimously objected.

They felt that it would be many years before the telecommunications industry had switched totally over to the new equipment and that personnel turnover at many companies using the older equipment would continue to result in a need for LDX training services. Besides, the new systems were being produced by overseas competitors of the old AmCom, and they had set up their own low-cost training organizations in the U.S., often providing training as part of the overall systems price.   Besides, Jane's executives identified a wide variety of potential problems with the new systems and felt that after time, the new equipment would lose its appeal to buyers and they would go back to using the old and would once again need LDX training.

Jane appreciated their advice. She felt that it was an example of effective horizontal and participatory management. Unfortunately, she was still confronted with the fact that LDX was on the verge of losing money because they were now providing less training and many of the long-time employees were left with little to do. What could she do?   To fire anyone would totally destroy morale, result in less productivity, and probably cost more than it would save in wages because of the tradition of virtual lifetime employment inherited from AmCom.

Case Questions

1.   LDX TechnoSystems placed great emphasis on quality. Did LDX exemplify total quality management? Why or why not?

2.   One of the reasons LDX had a very rigid vertical management structure was to ensure quality. Why might that be a good idea? Why might it be a bad idea?

3.   Which management perspective is exemplified by LDX? Why do you feel that way? Is there any element of another management perspective also present at LDX? If so, how does it help or hurt LDX?

4.   Can you identify one possible element of a learning organization at LDX even if that element is not functioning as required for such an organization? What is it and why did you select it? If you couldn't identify such an element, explain why not.

Journal Entries

Directions
The student Study Guide will include a requirement that you keep a journal of your thoughts and actions relating to selected classroom discussions and corresponding chapter assignments from the text.

For selected class discussions and each chapter covered, you will log the following journal entries:

1.   A summary description of Chapter 2 class discussions.

2.   A brief description of one <u>personal</u> <u>management</u> <u>activity</u> relating to Chapter 2. The activity could include a description of how your family history has affected your management of your personal life.

3.   A brief description of one <u>managerial</u> <u>incident</u> you have encountered
      <u>at work</u> as it relates to Chapter 2. This incident may include a description
      of how your present or past employer does or doesn't practice the
      concepts of the learning organization.

4.   Reflections on the interrelationship of the class discussions and the
      out-of-class activities and incidents you have recorded in 2 and 3.

In this way, you will be reporting on and verifying to what degree what you have read in the text and experienced in the classroom matches the reality of your daily personal and business life.

Your goals will be to better understand how managers really get things done through planning, organizing, directing, and controlling resources and by interacting with the firm's outside environment.

Also, this journal will serve as a means of developing your own critical thinking ability as well as your writing skill.

1.   Summary of Class Discussion

_____

_____

_____

_____

_____

_____

_____

_____

_____

_____

_____

_____

_____

_____

_____

2.   Personal Management Activity

Activity 1 _____

_____

_____

_____

Description 1 _____

_____

_____

_____

3.   Managerial Incident Encountered

Incident 1 _____

_____

_____

_____

Description 1 _____

_____

_____

_____

4.   Reflections on Class Discussion as Related to:

Activity 1 _____

_____

_____

_____

_____

_____

_____

_____

Incident 1 _____

_____

_____

_____

_____

_____

_____

_____

Chapter 2 Answer Key

Matching

Question	Answer	Question	Answer
1	o	11	h
2	t	12	p
3	b	13	l
4	f	14	r
5	y	15	a
6	j	16	x
7	v	17	w
8	m	18	s
9	u	19	c
10	d	20	i

Multiple Choice

Question	Answer	Question	Answer
1	c	9	d
2	b	10	b
3	a	11	d
4	d	12	a
5	b	13	d
6	c	14	b
7	a	15	c
8	c		

CHAPTER 3—THE ENVIRONMENT AND CORPORATE CULTURE

Chapter Outline	Corresponding Learning Objectives
I. The External Environment • General Environment • Task Environment	L.O. 1 Describe the general and task environments and the dimensions of each.
II. The Organization-Environment Relationship • Environmental Uncertainty • Adapting to the Environment • Influencing the Environment	L.O. 2 Explain how organizations adapt to an uncertain environment and identify techniques managers use to influence and control the external environment.
III. The Internal Environment: Corporate Culture • Symbols • Stories • Heroes • Slogans • Ceremonies	L.O. 3 Define corporate culture and give organizational examples. L.O. 4 Explain organizational symbols, stories, heroes, slogans, and ceremonies and how they relate to corporate culture.
IV. Environment and Culture • Adaptive Cultures • Types of Cultures	L.O. 5 Describe how corporate culture relates to the environment.
V. Shaping Corporate Culture for the Twenty-First Century • Changing and Merging Corporate Cultures • Symbolic Leadership	L.O. 6 Define a symbolic leader and explain the tools a symbolic leader uses to change corporate culture.

Major Concepts

(1) Organizational success involves successful interaction with an uncertain general and task environment. (2) Successful interaction involves not only changing the organization so as to adapt favorably to the environment but also using influencing techniques to change the environment so that it will be more favorable to the organization. (3) One of the best ways to effectively interact with the environment is to use the factors of its organizational culture to produce a culture that is adaptive and of the type that can meet the challenges of the twenty-first century.

In your own words, *what did the above paragraph say*? Perhaps the following will help you translate the above and strengthen your understanding of the third chapter!

First Sentence: Interaction with an Uncertain General and Task Environment
Uncertainties exist in both the general and task environments. Changes in the technological, sociocultural, economic, legal-political, and international dimensions of the general environment create both opportunities and threats for the organization. The same is true for changes in such elements of the task environment as its customers, competitors, suppliers, and its labor market. If a manager is to truly manage, the person must do more than passively recognize the existence and importance of the two environments. As covered immediately below, the manager may adapt the firm to the environment, change the environment so that it will adapt to the firm, or do some of both.

Second Sentence: Changing the Organization and Changing the Environment
Even if you can't change the world surrounding the organization, you may be able to change the organization so that it can adapt to its environment. Adaptation may be achieved by using those who have roles that span the organizational boundary such as those sales and marketing people who deal with outsiders, by using those whose planning and forecasting roles require an analysis of the environment, by developing a flexible organization that is capable of adapting to a changing environment, and by using mergers and joint ventures that force older organizational members to work with those who were previously outsiders. Of course, it can be a lot easier to adapt to the environment if you help change that environment so that it will be more favorable to your organization.

Techniques to influence change in the environment include advertising and public relations, political activities, and trade associations. Advertising is intended to change the environment in various ways: it hopefully will result in more sales than would have been the case otherwise by making people aware of the benefits involved in what you are selling; but, just as advertising can sell products or services to customers, it may also sometimes sell ideas to the general public.

Public relations can help engineer events and activities that may yield favorable publicity and favorable opinions on the part of the general public. Political activities include presenting your organization's side to political leaders on various issues that affect the organization—after all, why should only those who oppose you be heard?

Trade associations enable firms from throughout an industry to work together in bringing about environmental changes of common interest to all members.

Third Sentence: Culture—Adaptive, Types, and the Twenty-First Century

Culture is the set of key values, beliefs, understandings, and norms shared by members of an organization. An insight into an organization's culture can be obtained by examining such factors as organizational symbols (objects, acts, events), stories of true events that are repeatedly shared by members, heroes such as a dynamic CEO, slogans that express a key corporate value, and ceremonies such as awards ceremonies.

By working at improving these factors, one may also improve the organizational culture. In fact, organizational success may be dependent on its ability to maintain a culture that is adaptive to the environment and able to change its type of culture for management itself. Types of management cultures include club cultures, which stress long-term managerial careers and promotion from within but involve a variety of career experiences to provide a broader view of the organization; the academy culture, which is similar but stresses greater specialization for its managers; and the fortress culture, which characterizes organizations that are retrenching, downsizing, and seeking to turnaround—a threatening culture that does provide opportunity for any who can produce a turnaround.

The twenty-first century requires cultures that can not only adapt to changing realities but can adapt to other organizational cultures as needed, for example, in the case of a merger. The type of leader who can produce that type of outcome is the leader who knows how to effectively use the factors we discussed above: symbols, stories, slogans, and ceremonies.

Key Term Identification/Application

Matching Questions

Match each statement or situation with the key term that best describes it. (Note: Some terms will not be used.)

a.	organizational environment		p.	organic structure
b.	general environment		q.	mechanistic structure
c.	task environment		r.	merger
d.	internal environment		s.	joint venture
e.	international dimension		t.	political activity
f.	technological dimension		u.	trade association
g.	sociocultural dimension		v.	culture
h.	economic dimension		w.	symbol
i.	legal-political environment		x.	story
j.	pressure group		y.	hero
k.	customers		z.	slogan
l.	competitors		aa.	ceremony
m.	suppliers		bb.	culture gap
n.	labor market		cc.	symbolic leader
o.	boundary-spanning roles			

_____ 1.   "Just do it."

_____ 2.   The people who are available for hire by the organization.

_____ 3.   All the elements existing outside the organization's boundaries that have the potential to affect it.

_____ 4.   Dave Thomas of Wendy's.

_____ 5.   Currently there are many groups that are operating within the legal and political framework in an attempt to influence cigarette companies to behave in a socially responsible manner.

_____ 6.   A manager who defines and uses signals and symbols to influence corporate culture.

_____ 7. That portion of the external environment that consists of events originating in foreign countries.

_____ 8. Yesterday all the employees were called together to see Herman receive the Employee of the Year trophy, which is given to the employee that best provides customer service.

_____ 9. Those roles that are assumed by people that link and coordinate the organization with key elements of the external environment.

_____ 10. Every new employee is told about how Louise rented a helicopter, on her own, in order to deliver a customer's package on time.

_____ 11. The environment within the organization's boundaries.

_____ 12. Many governmental agencies have an organizational structure that is characterized by rigidly defined tasks, many rules and regulations, little teamwork, and centralized decision making.

_____ 13. That dimension of the general environment that represents the demographics, values, and norms of the population within which the organization operates.

_____ 14. The combination of two or more organizations into one.

_____ 15. The key values, beliefs, understandings, and norms that members of an organization share.

_____ 16. Anyone, people or organizations, who acquires goods or services from the organization.

_____ 17. The difference between an organization's desired norms and values and the actual norms and values.

_____ 18. That layer of the external environment that directly influences the organization's operations and performance.

_____ 19. Some organizations have an organizational structure that is free flowing, with few rules and regulations, which encourages employee teamwork and decentralized decision making.

_____ 20. People and organizations that provide the raw materials the organization uses to produce its outputs.

Multiple-Choice Questions

Consider the following situations and, utilizing the appropriate management concepts, answer the multiple-choice questions that follow.

Situation #1

Scott Johnson is an agent for a well-known shoe manufacturer. He has a large area of responsibility to contend with and his customers are well-known department stores. He is responsible for establishing contracts between the manufacturer and the retailer.

1.   Scott has discovered that the long-term forecast for the price of gasoline will be a 20 cent increase over the next six months. The manufacturer ships most of the shoes via truck. This rise in the price of gasoline is part of the:

      a.   task environment.
      b.   economic dimension.
      c.   technological dimension.
      d.   internal environment.

2.   Scott's general environment while serving as an agent for the shoe manufacturer is composed of:

      a.   the technological dimension.
      b.   the sociocultural dimension.
      c.   the economic dimension.
      d.   all of the above.

3.   Scott has recently learned that the shoe manufacturer that he represents outsources much of the raw material processing to a company in a lesser developed country, and that country is in the process of being battered by the largest typhoon in thirty years. This situation is part of the manufacturer's:

      a.   task environment.
      b.   legal-political dimension.
      c.   international dimension.
      d.   technological dimension.

4.   Scott is aware of a domestic interest group that would establish tariffs against any shoe company or companies producing part of a shoe from importing shoes into the United States over the next five years. This would enable the domestic shoe manufacturers to develop production processes that would rival the cheap cost of labor in foreign markets. This interest group is a/an:

   a.   pressure group.
   b.   competitor.
   c.   supplier.
   d.   customer.

5.   The shoe manufacturer's customers, suppliers, competitors, and labor market are all part of its:

   a.   general environment.
   b.   task environment.
   c.   internal environment.
   d.   none of the above.

Situation #2

Pramillia D'Souza is a manager for WE R XPRESS, an organization that positively guarantees the delivery of any package anywhere in the world within twenty-four hours. They are facing fierce competition for business and for survival.

6.   This fierce competition is part of the organization's:

   a.   general environment.
   b.   internal environment.
   c.   task environment.
   d.   sociocultural environment.

7.   In this environment of intense and fierce competition, with quick and innovative responses required of all employees from the CEO on down, which organizational structure would be most appropriate?

   a.   mechanistic.
   b.   bureaucratic.
   c.   hierarchial.
   d.   organic.

8.   Pramillia has often heard that there is strength in numbers. In order to counter some of the negative legislation aimed at the common-carrier overnight-package delivery industry, her company may want to join a/an:

    a.   trade association.
    b.   political party.
    c.   organic structure.
    d.   joint venture.

9.   If WE R XPRESS and RAPIDELIVERY wanted to simplify the situation and gain market coverage while eliminating some overhead cost, they could consider a/an:

    a.   trade association.
    b.   boundary spanning role.
    c.   joint venture.
    d.   merger.

10.   WE R XPRESS and RAPIDELIVERY are announcing on Monday that they will be cooperating in the funding and operation of a fleet of ships to be used by the competitors for operational purposes. This cooperation is known as a/an:

    a.   merger.
    b.   joint venture.
    c.   trade association.
    d.   technological dimension.

11.   The driving force behind WE R XPRESS has always been the unwavering commitment to customer service and the dedication to the principle of doing whatever it takes to deliver the package—whatever the cost. This commitment, dedication, and customer service orientation are a significant part of the organization's:

    a.   culture gap.
    b.   slogan.
    c.   culture.
    d.   ceremony.

12.   At RAPIDELIVERY, the story is different. While they have always strongly emphasized customer service in all of their literature, the truth is the organization has a stronger commitment to profits, growth, and market share. This difference at RAPIDELIVERY is :

    a.   culture gap.
    b.   organizational culture.
    c.   symbolic leadership.
    d.   political activity.

13.   On the last day of December, the president of WE R XPRESS turns the keys of a brand new sports car over to the employee who has best displayed the WE R XPRESSIVE! attitude in customer service and satisfaction. This activity is:

    a. symbolic leadership.
    b. a story.
    c. a ceremony.
    d. hero worship.

14.   If any merger were to occur between the two corporations, top management should identify a:

    a.   slogan.
    b.   hero.
    c.   story
    d.   symbolic leader.

15.   Pramillia's contact with organizational customers and suppliers has finally been positively recognized. This behavior on her part is known as:

    a.   a symbol.
    b.   a boundary-spanning role.
    c.   a hero.
    d.   political activity.

Skill Practice Exercises

Just-Suppose Scenarios

Scenario #1

Just suppose that one of your best friends has advised you to seek and pursue career options that will allow you to do the things that you enjoy doing. One of the many things that you enjoy doing is eating frozen yogurt. After several tries, you have managed to "land" a job as an assistant manager for one of the countries largest frozen yogurt chains.

1.   Identify and discuss the various elements of the general environment and the impact that they will have for you. Be specific!

2.   Identify and discuss the various specific elements of the task environment and their effect.

3.   Does an organic or mechanistic organizational structure make the most sense for you? Justify your answer.

Scenario #2

Just suppose that a few years have passed and now you are the district manager and in charge of 14 yogurt stores. One of the things that you have always taken pride in is that your stores emphasize teamwork, employee empowerment, and decentralized decision making.

1.   Describe your organization in terms of structure.

2.   Describe your organization in terms of culture.

3.   What conclusions can you draw from the above descriptions?

Scenario #3

Just suppose that you discover that your company is considering a horizontal merger with one of your primary competitors in order to enlarge market share and cut costs. This other organization has always been known to have centralized decision making, many rules and regulations, little teamwork, and rigidly defined tasks.

1.   Describe the "other" organization in terms of organizational structure and corporate culture.

2.   As this is of great concern to you, you have decided to become a symbolic leader. Describe and explain what this means, and how it applies to the current situation.

3.   Develop a key phrase or sentence that expresses the corporate values that you will attempt to carry over through the merger as a symbolic leader.

Personal Learning Experience

Application

Choose an organization that you have worked for, or the current or most recent college or university that you have attended, and describe the following:

A.   The general environment of that organization.

B.   The task environment of that organization.

C.   The organizational culture of that organization.

Integrated Case

The Merger Solution

LDX TechnoSystems was gaining competitors and losing customers. However, the organization had sufficient prestige and customers who still needed their training services. They provided training on telecommunications equipment that was actually a specialized form of a computer. Their profits were declining, but they had not yet lost money, and they had a substantial reserve of funds. Jane, their CEO, had an idea.

Why not takeover XV Enterprises, a small computer manufacturer that was on the verge of bankruptcy and thus available at relatively small cost? It could produce whatever telecommunications equipment businesses might want to buy, and LDX could provide the training services for that equipment. After all, LDX did have idle space and some underutilized employees available for such training.

Because of its prestige and Jane Rand's daring vision, LDX had little trouble in borrowing the money needed to acquire XV. LDX now had a substantial amount of debt, but it also had a new opportunity. Jane's move was such a surprise to the business community that it was covered in most major business periodicals, thus providing virtually free advertising for the products it planned to introduce. Through contacts in the government, she was able to engineer an antitrust investigation of those who would be her competitors, thus hoping to further strengthen her position as she began producing her own equipment.

After absorbing XV, Jane felt it was necessary to absorb XV people into LDX's culture. She felt that it was important for those at XV to now think of themselves as LDX.

As a result, she replaced many XV managers with LDX managers so that everyone throughout the now larger LDX would share the same values, beliefs, understandings, and norms. She got rid of old XV symbols and began using LDX slogans repeatedly at the former XV facilities. Through various meetings, she made the people at XV aware of LDX's heroic figures and some of the fascinating stories in its history. All ceremonies were conducted as LDX ceremonies.

Case Questions

1.   What challenges did Jane confront in the task environment?

2.   Explain how Jane attempted to change the environment and critique that attempt.

3.   What are the pros and cons of Jane's attempt to change organizational culture at the former XV Enterprises?

4.   How would you go about trying to produce an effective integrated culture for the merged XV and LDX?

Journal Entries

Directions

The Study Guide will include a requirement that you keep a journal of your thoughts and actions relating to selected classroom discussions and corresponding chapter assignments from the text.

For selected class discussions and each chapter covered, you will log the following journal entries:

1.   A summary description of Chapter 3 class discussions.

2.   A brief description of one <u>personal</u> <u>management</u> <u>activity</u> relating to Chapter 3. The activity could include a description of how you, in your personal time management, deal with an uncertain environment.

3.   A brief description of one <u>managerial</u> <u>incident</u> you have encountered <u>at work</u> as it relates to Chapter 3. This incident may include a look at your manager and how he or she does or does not demonstrate the definition of a symbolic leader.

4.   Reflections on the interrelationship of the class discussions and the out-of-class activity and incident you have recorded in 2 and 3.

In this way, you will be reporting on and verifying to what degree what you have read in the text and experienced in the classroom matches the reality of your daily personal and business life.

Your goals will be to better understand how managers really get things done through planning, organizing, leading, and controlling resources and by interacting with the firm's outside environment.

Also, this journal will serve as a means of developing your own critical thinking ability as well as your writing skill.

1.   Summary of Class Discussion

_____

_____

_____

_____

_____

_____

_____

_____

_____

_____

_____

_____

_____

_____

2.   Personal Management Activity

Activity 1 _____

_____

_____

_____

Description 1 _____

_____

_____

_____

3.   Managerial Incident Encountered

Incident 1 _____

_____

_____

_____

Description 1 _____

_____

_____

_____

4.   Reflections on Class Discussion as Related to:

Activity 1 _____

_____

_____

_____

_____

_____

_____

_____

_____

Incident 1 _____

_____

_____

_____

_____

_____

_____

Chapter 3 Answer Key

Matching

Question	Answer	Question	Answer
1	z	11	d
2	n	12	q
3	a	13	g
4	y	14	r
5	j	15	v
6	cc	16	k
7	e	17	bb
8	aa	18	c
9	o	19	p
10	x	20	m

Multiple Choice

Question	Answer	Question	Answer
1	b	9	d
2	d	10	b
3	c	11	c
4	a	12	a
5	b	13	c
6	c	14	d
7	d	15	b
8	a		

CHAPTER 4—MANAGING IN A GLOBAL ENVIRONMENT

Chapter Outline	Corresponding Learning Objectives
I. A Borderless World	L.O. 1 Describe the emerging borderless world.
II. The International Business Environment	L.O. 2 Define international management and explain how it differs from the management of domestic business operations.
III. The Economic Environment	L.O. 3 Indicate how dissimilarities in the economic, sociocultural, and legal-political environments throughout the world can affect business operations.
IV. The Legal-Political Environment • General Agreement on Tariffs and Trade • European Union • North American Free Trade Agreement (NAFTA) • Trade Alliances: Promise or Pitfall?	
V. The Sociocultural Environment	
VI. Getting Started Internationally • Outsourcing • Exporting • Licensing • Direct Investing	L.O. 4 Describe market-entry strategies that businesses use to develop foreign markets.
VII. The Multinational Corporation • Characteristics of Multinational Corporations	L.O. 5 Describe the characteristics of a multinational corporation and the generic strategies available to it.
VIII. Managing in a Global Environment • Personal Challenges for Global Managers • Managing Cross-Culturally • Global Learning	L.O. 6 Explain the strategic approaches used by multinational corporations.

Major Concepts

(1) The international business environment has economic, legal-political, and sociocultural environment dimensions that will affect the organization that is getting started and is expanding in global business. (2) Starting and expanding globally may include outsourcing, exporting, licensing, and direct investing. (3) Managing the multinational corporation involves personal and cross-cultural challenges that require continuous learning.

In your own words, *what did the above paragraph say*? Perhaps the following will help you translate the above and strengthen your understanding of the fourth chapter!

First Sentence: Economic, Legal-Political, and Sociocultural Dimensions
Whether to do business in a particular country may be affected by economic considerations. For example, what is the level of its economic development—i.e., what is its per capita income and how does that affect market potential? Does the country have the needed infrastructure for you to do business—i.e., what is the state of its highways, electric power, communication facilities, etc.? Will it be able to obtain the specific resources needed to take advantage of the product markets? What about the country's currency? Currency issues involve the extent to which the corporation can convert the foreign currency into U.S. currency and the predictability as to how the rate of exchange may change over time.

The legal-political environment of a country includes political risks such as the possibility that a government may seize the organization's assets. It includes political instability such as riots and revolutions. It also involves changing laws and regulations as well as how they are enforced. The General Agreement on Tariffs and Trade (GATT) has endeavored to improve the legal-political environment for trade and to reduce trade barriers around the world. The European Union and the North American Free Trade Agreement (NAFTA) go beyond GATT and focus on improving trade within specific areas of the world.

The sociocultural environment of a nation includes social values such as the extent to which people accept inequality (known as "power distance"), seek to avoid uncertainty, tend to focus on individual accomplishment and responsibility versus collective accomplishment and responsibility, and so-called "masculinity/femininity" attributes. "Masculinity" refers to preference for achievement, assertiveness, focus on work, material success, etc., whereas "femininity" refers to valuing relationships, cooperation, group decision making, and quality of life. Other sociocultural characteristics include the existence of multiple languages and ethnocentrism—the tendency to view one's own culture as superior to others.

Second Sentence: Outsourcing, Exporting, Licensing, and Direct Investing

The world outside of one's home country provides additional opportunities for supplies as well as sales; one often can take advantage of these opportunities without a significant overseas investment.

Organizations that no longer wish to produce something themselves may wish to consider outsourcing the production to an overseas firm instead of a domestic producer.   In addition to selling one's products in U.S. markets, one may wish to export the product for sales in overseas markets as well.

Licensing also provides a way to take advantage of international opportunities in a way that may require little or no investment overseas.   Basically it involves allowing organizations overseas to produce and/or distribute your products.

Direct investment means actually acquiring overseas resources such as production and distribution facilities to conduct your business in various countries.

Third Sentence: Multinationals, Cross-Cultural and Personal Challenges, Learning

A multinational corporation operates under a single authority and may be based in a particular nation, but all of its worldwide activities are integrated into a single stateless, borderless, integrated system. As a result, the existence of managers and employees who have cross-cultural capabilities to interact and manage can be a major plus for such corporations. Managers in international organizations have a personal challenge in being able to adapt and adjust management principles to varying cultures; for example, what may motivate people in one culture may demotivate people in another culture.   As a result, global managers must be continual learners, developing an awareness of various cultures and staying in touch with changes developing in those cultures.

Key Term Identification/Application

Matching Questions

Match each statement or situation with the key term that best describes it. (Note: Some terms will not be used.)

a.	international management	m.	market-entry strategy
b.	infrastructure	n.	global outsourcing
c.	political risk	o.	exporting
d.	most favored nation	p.	countertrade
e.	culture	q.	licensing
f.	power distance	r.	franchising
g.	uncertainty avoidance	s.	direct investing
h.	individualism	t.	joint venture
i.	collectivism	u.	wholly owned foreign affiliate
j.	masculinity		
k.	femininity	v.	greenfield venture
l.	ethnocentrism	w.	multinational corporation (MNC)

_____ 1.   Jones has decided to build a subsidiary from scratch in a foreign company, which is the riskiest type of direct investment.

_____ 2.   All of a country's physical facilities, such as roads and bridges, which support economic activities.

_____ 3.   The barter of products for other products rather than selling them for currency.

_____ 4.   Most Americans do not tend to accept inequalities in power among institution, organizations, or people.

_____ 5.   We all know that our American culture is better than any other culture in the world.

_____ 6.   Organizations need to develop a strategy for entering foreign markets.

_____ 7.   The management of business operations conducted in more than one country.

_____ 8.   Some organizations simply maintain their American facilities and sell their products in foreign markets.

_____ 9.   The most favorable treatment that a country can grant any other country in terms of imports and exports.

_____ 10.   Any organization that receives more than 25 percent of its total revenues from operations outside the parent company's home country.

_____ 11.   Some Japanese automakers are involved in managing their production facilities in America.

_____ 12.   Some societies show a strong preference for cooperation, group decision making, and quality of life.

_____ 13.   Some Canadian countries make certain resources available to companies in Ireland in order to participate in the production and sale of its products there.

_____ 14.   The shared knowledge, beliefs, values, behaviors, and ways of thinking among members of society.

_____ 15.   A Swedish and an American company are sharing the costs and risks in order to build some new fish hatcheries.

_____ 16.   Most Americans have a fairly loose-knit social framework in that they realize that individuals are expected to take care of themselves.

_____ 17.   A foreign subsidiary over which an organization has complete control.

_____ 18.   Many American companies have decided not to invest in many of the African countries due to the risk of losing their assets, earning power, or managerial control due to the politics of the area.

_____ 19.   Often companies seek the cheapest source of labor and supplies, regardless of country or location, in the production of the product.

_____ 20.   We often show that we have a strong cultural preference for achievement, heroism, assertiveness, and material success.

Multiple-Choice Questions

Consider the following situations and, utilizing the appropriate management concepts, answer the multiple-choice questions that follow.

Situation #1

During your college days, you are given the incredible opportunity of serving a six-month internship in the Far East for an internationally known petroleum company.

1.   During your visits to some of the Asian cities, you are struck by the lack of sanitation and the flimsiness of the housing. As far as you are concerned, these cities and societies must be crude and uncivilized. You are showing your:

     a.   low power distance.
     b.   high tolerance for ambiguity
     c.   ethnocentrism.
     d.   masculinity.

2.   Some of the countries have very poor roads by which to transport goods or people and a nonexistent pipeline system. You are very concerned about the:

     a.   power distance.
     b.   infrastructure.
     c.   ethnocentrism.
     d.   individualism.

3.   You are very concerned about the risk of losing company assets and power in a city such as Hong Kong, which has recently reverted to Chinese rule. This concern centers around the concept of:

     a.   ethnocentrism.
     b.   infrastructure.
     c.   masculinity.
     d.   political risk.

4. You are also amazed by not only the great wealth of the area but also the abject poverty. There is a tremendous difference between the "haves" and the "have nots," and the society seems to accept this. You are examining that society's:

    a. power distance.
    b. uncertainty avoidance.
    c. individualism.
    d. collectivism.

5. In some of the lesser developed countries, there seems to be a stronger emphasis on and preference for a tightly knit social framework in which individuals look after one another than exists in the more developed countries. This is the aspect of culture called:

    a. individualism.
    b. collectivism.
    c. uncertainty avoidance.
    d. power distance.

6. With your six-month internship almost over, you realize that one of the strongest aspects of American culture, as opposed to Asian culture, is that Americans are always striving for achievement, they believe in heros, and they value assertiveness and material success. This aspect of culture is called:

    a. individualism.
    b. femininity.
    c. masculinity.
    d. ethnocentrism.

Situation #2

After you returned to college, you talked with several of the other international interns concerning their experiences.

7. One of the interns worked for a company that receives more than 25 percent of its revenues from its foreign operations. This company is a/an:

    a. multinational corporation (MNC).
    b. global corporation.
    c. transnational corporation.
    d. all of the above.

8.   Another student worked for an organization that bought grain and soybeans from American farmers and sold them to foreign markets. This market-entry strategy is called:

    a.   exporting.
    b.   countertrade.
    c.   franchising.
    d.   a joint venture.

9.   Other students worked for an organization in the textile industry. The organization actively sought the cheapest sources of materials and labor for the processing of their clothes, regardless of country or location. This is called:

    a.   countertrade.
    b.   franchising.
    c.   global outsourcing.
    d.   a joint venture.

10.   A student who worked for a tractor manufacturer was amazed to report that the company traded tractors for raw materials such as zinc and iron ore. This arrangement is called:

    a.   exporting.
    b.   countertrade.
    c.   global outsourcing.
    d.   a joint venture.

Situation #3

With the demise of Communism in Russia and the entry of Russia into NATO, many companies, including your fast-food restaurant chain, are sensing tremendous economic opportunities.

11.   Your organization has decided to pay for the promotion of the chain in order to help participate in the production and sale of their products. This strategy is called:

    a.   licensing.
    b.   franchising.
    c.   countertrade.
    d.   direct investing.

12.	Next year your organization is considering entering into contractual arrangements with foreign companies that will purchase the rights to distribute your product and services in that country. This arrangement is called:

	a.	a joint venture.
	b.	franchising.
	c.	licensing.
	d.	exporting.

13.	If your other strategies are successful, the organization has already determined that it will open several of its own facilities with American management. This strategy is called:

	a.	exporting.
	b.	licensing.
	c.	franchising.
	d.	direct investing.

14.	One of the very important aspects of your business is ensuring that the infrastructure of the country will support the distribution of your products and raw materials. Your organization has decided to share the costs and risks of developing three centrally located meat processing facilities. This activity is called a/an:

	a.	wholly owned foreign affiliate.
	b.	greenfield venture.
	c.	joint venture.
	d.	countertrade.

15.	Your brother has always been a risk taker and has decided, after seeing the tremendous success of your organization in Europe, to open his own pizza chain from scratch in Africa. This strategy is called:

	a.	a greenfield venture.
	b.	a joint venture.
	c.	licensing.
	d.	franchising.

Skill Practice Exercises

Just-Suppose Scenarios

Scenario #1

Just suppose that you have been hired as a sales-associate trainee for one of the leading international software-development organizations. Your first assignment is in India.

1.   Based upon what you know, evaluate India in terms of infrastructure, political risk, and culture.

2.   Are there any special barriers to women or minorities in India?

3.   Describe the Indian culture in terms of power distance, individualism, and masculinity/femininity.

Scenario #2

Just suppose that your organization is a high-quality producer of a variety of plastics. As the Vice President of Operations, you are responsible for identifying and developing a successful market-entry strategy.

1.   Explain how you would utilize the strategy of global outsourcing or global sourcing.

2.   Justify the choice of exporting as an appropriate market-entry strategy.

3.   How would a countertrade agreement work for you?

Scenario #3

Just suppose that you are the Operation's Manager for an aggressive and growing organization that specializes in the manufacture of farm equipment. You are evaluating appropriate market-entry strategies.

1.   Describe the usefulness of licensing and/or franchising to your organization.

2.   Would a strategy of direct investing be appropriate? Why or why not?

3.   What would be the riskiest strategy to utilize? Would you recommend this? Justify your answer.

Personal Learning Experience

Library/Internet Research

Utilizing your local library or the Internet, research at least three sources that discuss market-entry strategies.

1.   Discuss the various strategies that are currently being utilized.

2.   From what you currently know about market-entry strategies, how would you evaluate these strategies?

3.   Are you prepared to work for a multinational corporation? Which skills do you need to develop, based upon your research?

Integrated Case

Global Expansion

Most of LDX TechnoSystems's customers were in the U.S., but their CEO, Jane Rand, felt that a growing global market for telecommunications equipment provided an exciting opportunity for LDX. LDX began looking for suppliers outside the U.S. The company wanted to establish itself in the export market, but that market was already dominated by larger and better known firms; therefore, LDX picked out areas of the world that the larger firms had overlooked, in particular, nations that were currently poor and somewhat limited on funds.

Jane felt by demonstrating her company's confidence in those nations, she would establish a loyal overseas customer base that would become very valuable as those countries began to grow their economies. Unfortunately, the sales LDX made were in local currencies, which were almost impossible to convert into dollars. As a result, she used the currencies within the nations to build production facilities. Those facilities would be close to other overseas markets she was trying to reach.

In some overseas locations, the local governments were especially helpful to LDX in setting up operations, because LDX seemed to offer the potential economic growth needed to reduce rising unrest on the part of the poorest segments of the population.

Because local citizens in the countries feared foreign domination, she trained local employees for all employment positions in the facilities, including top management.

Another reason she trained locals was their resistance to the LDX managers she had sent overseas. Those U.S. managers used the same techniques that had previously enabled them to be very successful, but it seemed that local employees just did not wish to respond or learn U.S. ways of doing things.

Case Questions

1.   Discuss the political risks in Jane's international strategy.

2.   Discuss the pros and cons of LDX's selection of the economic environment in which it plans to do business.

3.   Has LDX become a truly multinational corporation? Why or why not?

4.   Discuss LDX's cross-cultural and personal-management challenges.

Journal Entries

Directions
The Study Guide will include a requirement that you keep a journal of your thoughts and actions relating to selected classroom discussions and corresponding chapter assignments from the text.

For selected class discussions and each chapter covered, you will log the following journal entries:

1.   A summary description of Chapter 4 class discussions.

2.   A brief description of one <u>personal</u> <u>management</u> <u>activity</u> relating to Chapter 4. The activity could include how the global environment affects your purchasing patterns.

3.   A brief description of one <u>managerial</u> <u>incident</u> you have encountered <u>at work</u> as it relates to Chapter 4. This incident may include a look at how your company views foreign competition for its product or services.

4.   Reflections on the interrelationship of the class discussions and the out-of-class activity and incident you have recorded in 2 and 3.

In this way, you will be reporting on and verifying to what degree what you have read in the text and experienced in the classroom matches the reality of your daily personal and business life.

Your goals will be to better understand how managers really get things done through planning, organizing, leading, and controlling resources and by interacting with the firm's outside environment.

Also, this journal will serve as a means of developing your own critical thinking ability as well as your writing skill.

1.   Summary of Class Discussion

_____

_____

_____

_____

_____

_____

_____

_____

_____

_____

_____

_____

_____

_____

_____

2.   Personal Management Activity

Activity 1 _____

_____

_____

_____

Description 1 _____

_____

_____

_____

3.   Managerial Incident Encountered

Incident 1 _____

_____

_____

_____

Description 1 _____

_____

_____

_____

4.   Reflections on Class Discussion as Related to:

Activity 1 _____

_____

_____

_____

_____

_____

_____

_____

_____

Incident 1 _____

_____

_____

_____

_____

_____

_____

Chapter 4 Answer Key

Matching

Question	Answer	Question	Answer
1	v	11	s
2	b	12	k
3	p	13	q
4	f	14	e
5	l	15	t
6	m	16	h
7	a	17	u
8	o	18	c
9	d	19	n
10	w	20	j

Multiple Choice

Question	Answer	Question	Answer
1	c	9	c
2	b	10	b
3	d	11	a
4	a	12	b
5	b	13	d
6	c	14	c
7	d	15	a
8	a		

CHAPTER 5—MANAGEMENT ETHICS AND CORPORATE SOCIAL RESPONSIBILITY

Chapter Outline	Corresponding Learning Objectives
I. What Is Managerial Ethics?	L.O. 1 Define ethics and explain how ethical behavior relates to behavior governed by law and free choice.
II. Criteria for Ethical Decision Making • Utilitarian Approach • Individialism Approach • Leading • Controlling	L.O. 2 Explain the utilitarian individualism, moral-rights, and justice approaches for evaluating ethical behavior.
III. Factors Affecting Ethical Choices • The Manager • The Organization	L.O. 3 Describe how both individual and organizational factors shape ethical decision making.
IV. What Is Social Responsibility?	
V. Organizational Stakeholders	
VI. The Natural Environment	L.O. 4 Define corporate social responsibility and how to evaluate it along economic, legal, ethical, and discretionary criteria.
VII. Evaluating Corporate Social Performance • Economic Responsibilities • Legal Responsibilities • Ethical Responsibilities • Discretionary Responsibilities	
VIII. Corporate Actions toward Social Demands	L.O. 5 Describe four corporate responses to social demands.
	L.O. 6 Explain the concept of stakeholder and identify important stakeholders for organizations.
IX. Managing Company Ethics and Social Responsibility	L.O. 7 Describe structures managers can use to improve their organizations' ethics and social responsiveness.
X. Ethics and the Management Revolution.	

Major Concepts

(1) Managerial ethics falls between the legal code and the area of complete free choice, but there is no single criterion or approach used to determine what is ethical in any given situation. (2) The choice as to what is ethical may be affected by the characteristics of the manager or the organization. (3) Today, managers are being urged to make choices based on their social responsibility to stakeholders and the natural environment. (4) Today, many are urging that the evaluation of management include a consideration of how it has performed relative to its social responsibilities and its responsiveness to demands for improved ethics and social responsibility.

In your own words, *what did the above paragraph say*? Perhaps the following will help you translate the above and strengthen your understanding of the fifth chapter!

First Sentence: Ethics and Ethical Criteria

Ethics is the code of moral principles and values that governs the behaviors of a person or group with respect to what is right or wrong. It falls within the area between codified law and free choice. Just because an action does not violate a law does not mean that it is ethical; there may well be nongovernmental expectations as to what should or should not be done in a given situation and nongovernmental punishments involved for failure to do that which is ethical. Actions falling within free choice involve those in which there are no such significant expectations.

One reason controversies may develop as to what is ethical is due to the varied criteria that may be used for making ethical decisions. The criteria include the utilitarianism approach, which involves the greatest good for the greatest number (there can be problems as to what is the greatest good); the individualism approach, which stresses the importance of the individual (it does not necessarily ignore others because it recognizes that there could be problems if everyone looks out only for him or herself); the moral-rights approach, which asserts that certain rights exist for people, and they must not be violated by management; and the justice approach, which involves justice in terms of rules and/or in terms of the outcomes produced by actions.

Second Sentence: The Manager and the Organization

Some managers operate at the so-called preconventional level, in which the manager conforms to ethical standards only because he or she must do so to avoid punishments or obtain rewards, not because of any internal values and beliefs. At the second level, the conventional level, the manager will do that which is ethical because of his or her internal values and beliefs but will not necessarily always be willing to disobey higher management or suffer punishments in order to do that which is ethical. At the highest level, the postconventional or principled level, the manager will do that which is right even if it results in personal loss.

The organizational culture also varies as to the general level of commitment to ethics. One of the best ways to communicate the organization's commitment is through its actions, especially when the actions could be costly, such as Johnson & Johnson's response in the situation involving tampering with its Tylenol product.

Third Sentence: Stakeholders and the Natural Environment

The owners of a corporation are the stockholders; some managers feel that all management must focus only on what is good for the stockholders. Others feel that there are others who have a stake or interest in the business, and it is only fair that their interests should also be considered. These others include customers, suppliers, employees, and the local community. What may be good for one stakeholder may not always be good for others.

For example, the natural environment is an area of growing concern for many potential customers and other members of society.   However, not all customers share the concern to such a high level of dedication that they would be willing to pay more for a product if it is environmentally friendly. Furthermore, what may be good for the environment may not always be good for employment or the local community, which depends on that employment.

Fourth Sentence: Evaluating Performance and Responsiveness

Many feel that management must not be evaluated only on whether it has obeyed the law, because behavior that is legal is not always right. They   disagree with managers who feel that they must put the owner's interests first and feel that management should not only be willing to accept a lower return in order to maintain high ethical standards but should even go above and beyond ethical expectations—otherwise referred to as "discretionary responsibility. "   It has been suggested that when confronted with social demands, management has a range of possible responses from obstruction or resistance to being proactive or anticipating the demand and endeavoring to take action before being asked. Of course, there could be differences of opinion as to whether certain behavior should be labeled as obstructive or simply as an attempt by the organization to defend itself against something that is untrue or unnecessary.

Some of the ways that ethics may be improved include leadership by example, a formal code of ethics, ethical structures such as committees and ombudsmen, and the encouragement of whistle blowers.

Key Term Identification/Application

Matching Questions

Match each statement or situation with the key term that best describes it.

a.   ethics
b.   ethical dilemma
c.   utilitarian approach
d.   individualism approach
e.   moral-rights approach
f.   justice approach
g.   distributive justice
h.   procedural justice
i.   compensatory justice
j.   social responsibility

k.   stakeholder
l.   discretionary reponsibility
m.   obstructive response
n.   defensive response
o.   accommodative response
p.   proactive response
q.   code of ethics
r.   ethics committee
s.   ethics ombudsman
t.   whistle-blowing

_____ 1.   I could hire my best friend, who really needs the job, or another applicant whom I don't know, who is the best qualified for the job. I don't know which course of action is right or wrong.

_____ 2.   Any person or group within or outside the organization that has a stake in, or an interest in, the organization's performance.

_____ 3.   Recently one of my co-workers came forward and told the press of the bribes the organization was paying certain officials in Washington.

_____ 4.   Those moral principles and values that govern a person's or group's behavior when it comes to right or wrong.

_____ 5.   The Goldman family sued Jones for the cost of certain injuries that Jones inflicted on the Goldman family. Jones's only defense was that he didn't have any control over the situation, so he shouldn't be held responsible for it.

_____ 6.   One of the local insurance companies has discovered that a significant concern in the area is the teenage pregnancy problem. As a result of this knowledge and without any pressure from anyone, the organization has developed and implemented several programs that address the issue.

_____ 7.   Tanya believes that moral decisions should be based upon standards of equity, fairness, and impartiality.

_____ 8.   Simon and Lois are two of the executives on the committee that is assigned the responsibility of overseeing the organization's ethics. They rule on questionable issues and discipline violators.

_____ 9.   Often, business organizations take the approach that the best and most moral approach is the approach that produces the greatest good for the greatest number.

_____ 10.   When an employee starts work here, one of the first things that they do is to sign a statement that says that they have read and understood the organization's formal statement regarding its position on ethics and social issues.

_____ 11.   I believe that morals are personal and that the most moral approach is that which promotes the individual's best long-term interests. If everyone does this, then the greater good will be achieved.

_____ 12.   A new concert amphitheater claims that evidence of noise pollution is misleading and distorted, denies any responsibility for the noise pollution, and blocks any attempt to investigate the situation.

_____ 13.   Everything would be fine if all of our rules and procedures were clearly stated and consistently and impartially enforced.

_____ 14.   Over the last year, our organization has changed its position to one of admitting that some of our actions have been wrong and of not acting obstructively.

_____ 15.   The best and most moral of decisions are those that to the highest degree possible maintain the rights of those affected by them.

_____ 16.   Juanita has always been known to be a fair and level-headed person, so she has been given the responsibility for hearing and investigating ethics complaints and pointing out potential problems to top managers.

_____ 17.   People should not be treated differently based upon arbitrary characteristics, but if significant and substantive differences are found, then people should be treated differently in proportion to their differences.

_____ 18.   Our organization, after much media pressure, has accepted its social responsibility for its actions and has agreed to comply with the public interest.

_____ 19.   It is the obligation of the organization, and the organization's management, to make decisions and take actions that will enhance the welfare and interests of society as well as the organization.

_____ 20.   Ronald McDonald House is an example of an activity that was voluntary on the part of McDonald's and was not mandated by law, economics, or ethics, but simply by the organization's desire to make a social contribution.

Multiple-Choice Questions

Consider the following situations and, utilizing the appropriate management concepts, answer the multiple-choice questions that follow.

Situation #1

It is spring time and you are the General Manager of a landscaping company. This is your busy season and you have a tremendous amount of competition in your area. Your problem is that you have promised a local country club the delivery of several thousand flowers for an important event. Your Operations Manager has just made you aware that your company cannot provide the quality of product that the customer desires on time, but it is possible that you can adjust the order within a few weeks after delivery. Should you tell the customer the situation and risk losing the account to your competition, or keep quiet knowing that the customer will be irritated but will probably stick with you?

1.   This situation can best be described as a/an:

    a.   ethical dilemma.
    b.   discretionary responsibility.
    c.   whistle-blowing incident.
    d.   none of the above.

2.   Perhaps what is important is making a decision that will produce the greatest good for the greatest number, and with all the employees, stockholders, suppliers, and other stakeholders involved, it is clear that you should deliver the faulty-quality shipment. This is the:

    a.   individualism approach.
    b.   moral-rights approach.
    c.   utilitarian approach.
    d.   justice approach.

3.   Your spouse suggests that your decision should simply be based upon what is in your best long-term interest, since in the long-run this will result in the greater good. Your spouse has adopted the:

    a.   utilitarian approach.
    b.   individualism approach.
    c.   moral-rights approach.
    d.   justice approach.

4.   As you debate the subject, critical time is passing, and the president of the company pulls you into her office to talk with you. As you describe the situation, the president appears to be very focused and says, "Moral decisions must be based on standards of equity, fairness, and impartiality. Do what is right." This is the:

    a.   utilitarian approach.
    b.   individualism approach.
    c.   moral-rights approach.
    d.   justice approach.

5.   Your conclusion, after weighing all the possibilities, is that human beings have fundamental rights and one of those is the right of free consent, which means that individuals are to be treated only as they knowingly and freely consent to be treated. Thus, an ethically right decision is one that best maintains the rights of those people affected by it. You have settled on the:

    a.   utilitarian approach.
    b.   individualism approach.
    c.   moral-rights approach.
    d.   justice approach.

Situation #2

Several months later, you are faced with yet another ethical dilemma. Should you hire a good friend of your spouse or should you hire a more qualified person whom you do not know?

6.   You have decided to approach this situation from the justice approach; the only problem is, there are different types of justice! One type of justice insists that rules (in this case rules of hiring) should be clearly stated and consistently and impartially enforced. This is:

    a.   compensatory justice.
    b.   distributive justice.
    c.   procedural justice.
    d.   none of the above.

7.   You also think that judging someone on whether or not your spouse knows them is an arbitrary rather than substantive characteristic. This concept is at the core of:

    a.   compensatory justice.
    b.   distributive justice.
    c.   procedural justice.
    d.   none of the above.

8.   Which type of justice would maintain that if your decision were wrong and resulted in the injury of the parties, YOU should be responsible for the cost of those injuries?

    a.   compensatory justice.
    b.   distributive justice.
    c.   procedural justice.
    d.   none of the above.

9.   It would probably be very helpful to you and other employees of the company if the organization would produce a formal statement of the organization's values regarding ethics and social values. This statement is a/an:

    a.   obstructive response.
    b.   code of ethics.
    c.   accommodative response.
    d.   ethical dilemma.

10.   Because you are so concerned with these issues, and because they have so much impact on how you conduct business, you have decided to volunteer to be a member of the group of executives that oversees the organization's ethics by ruling on questions of ethics. You will be:

    a.   the ethics ombudsman.
    b.   a whistle-blower.
    c.   an ethics guru.
    d.   a member of the ethics committee.

Situation #3

Your company has been responsible for building a top-notch concert center in your town and attracting big-name entertainers to perform. Unfortunately, people living within a four-mile radius of your facility are complaining to the mayor about the loudness of the music and that it seems to go on all night.

11.   You are starting to realize that your business affects more than the owners of the business, the entertainers, and the customers. It also seems to affect the community, city government, and even suppliers of the concert center. You are starting to consider all of the:

    a.   stockholders.
    b.   cardholders.
    c.   stakeholders.
    d.   banner holders.

12.   Initially your company's position was to deny any wrongdoing and state that noise-level testing in the surrounding area has been inconclusive; also, at the same time, your company took active steps to prevent reporters, or others, from gathering actual data. This position is the:

    a.   discretionary response.
    b.   obstructive response.
    c.   defensive response.
    d.   proactive response.

13.   After two years of operation and considerable and constant public pressure, your organization has built a sound wall around the facility and has publicly acknowledged and accepted social responsibility for its actions. This is a/an:

    a.   accommodative response.
    b.   defensive response.
    c.   proactive response.
    d.   discretionary response.

14.   Recently the organization has been instrumental in developing sound-control systems that circulate the sound among the audience rather that drive the sound into the surrounding community. It is clear that your organization truly desires to make social contributions that are not being demanded or mandated by either economics, the law, or ethics. This is an example of:

    a.   the accommodative response.
    b.   the proactive response.
    c.   discretionary responsibility.
    d.   a code of ethics.

15.   As you sit in your office and contemplate the changes the organization has undergone in terms of social responsibility, you start wondering if there are community concerns, quite apart from noise and noise pollution, that the organization should be addressing without any community pressure. You are considering adopting a/an:

    a.   defensive response.
    b.   discretionary responsibility position.
    c.   accommodative response.
    d.   proactive response.

Skill Practice Exercises

Just-Suppose Scenarios

Scenario #1

Just suppose that you are a distributor of hospital products and have just been approached by the largest health-care provider in your state to submit a bid to them that would enable you to be the single largest provider of health-care products in the state. If you use a lower grade quality of materials than that specified in the contract, you know that you can underbid your competitors substantially. Should you do this?

1.   Examine this situation and your course of action from each of the following approaches:

        A.   Utilitarian Approach

        B.   Individualism Approach

        C.   Moral-Rights Approach

        D.   Justice Approach

2.   Which course of action will you choose?   Why?

Scenario #2

Just suppose that you are now working as a manager-in-training for one of the large cigarette-producing companies. Also realize that your company is not only one of the largest producers in the area, but also one of the largest employers in the area.

1.   Describe the various stakeholders in this situation. What is their "stake" or interest in the operation of the company?

2.   Describe the scale of responses to social demands that are available to the company.

3.   Which of the responses would you advocate and why?

Scenario #3

Just suppose that you have demonstrated good sales talent and have been hired as a used-car salesperson at the largest dealership in town. Success in this position will greatly enhance your career possibilities.

1.   Suppose that you knew of several unethical and borderline illegal activities that several salespersons were performing.   What is your ethical dilemma?

2.   If you do nothing, who does it affect?

3.   What will you do, and why? Which ethical approach have you utilized?

Personal Learning Experience

Interview

Contact a branch office of one of the major real-estate firms in your area. Ask for an appointment to talk with the broker, and explain that you are working on a school project.

1.   Ask the broker about the ethical issues or dilemmas that he/she faces in this business.

2.   What type of ethical training is provided for the real-estate associates?

3.   How does the broker recommend resolving ethical dilemmas?

4.   Evaluate the interview.

5.   Would you do business with this firm? Why or Why not?

Integrated Case

Unethical Ethics?

Soon after becoming CEO of LDX TechnoSystems, Jane Rand experimented in providing more empowerment to lower levels in the organization only to have her trust betrayed by one person who engaged in fraud. She ended the empowerment at the time, but she knew that her growing global organization would require more decisions to be made at lower levels. She was worried about the possibility that some managers would engage in unethical behavior that could embarrass LDX. As a result, she asked that all managers discuss business ethics with their employees. She also wanted the managers to urge employees to become whistle blowers if any observed unethical behavior.

She overheard one such discussion and was not pleased with what she heard. (The people in the meeting did not realize that she was in the area.) One person responded: "Business ethics? Isn't that an oxymoron like military intelligence?" Another said : "So Jane wants us to report any wrong-doing? What if she is doing wrong or the whole company is doing wrong? I think I could present very solid proof that the government has been overcharged on contracts. Should I blow the whistle to the Feds?" "Good point," said another. "I think the IRS would be interested in some additional details on the expenses listed by this company. May I have time off to take copies of the documents to the Federal Building downtown?"

Jane was not aware that there were any problems in regards to overcharging or tax deductions, but she felt that it was necessary to clarify her ethics policy and prevent any of the actions those employees seemed to be threatening. She asked her administrative assistant, Bill Williams, to help her draft a formal code of ethics.

She suggested that criteria be included in the code to help people identify that which is ethical and that which is not. In particular, she advocated that an action be judged as to whether it would be good or bad for the company. She felt that this criteria was in line with the utilitarian approach in that whatever was good for the company was good for the greatest number—i.e., all the stakeholders who were dependent on the company such as employees, members of the local community, etc.

She also wanted whistle blowing to focus on actions that involve fraud against the company. If any person feels that the company has done anything unethical, she wanted that to be reported to an ombudsman who would report directly to her. She felt that if anything is wrong at LDX, the company should first have the opportunity to deal with the problem before it gets outside the organization and possibly destroys the company.

Case Questions

1.   Discuss the extent to which Jane is recommending a utilitarian approach to ethics.

2.   What are the pros and cons of her approach to whistle blowing?

3.   To what extent does employee empowerment result in a greater or lesser need for a code of conduct?

4.   Compare Jane's approach to management ethics to the approach you would recommend and indicate the reasons for your recommendation.

Journal Entries

Directions

The Study Guide will include a requirement that you keep a journal of your thoughts and actions relating to selected classroom discussions and corresponding chapter assignments from the text.

For selected class discussions and each chapter covered, you will log the following journal entries:

1.   A summary description of Chapter 5 class discussions.

2.   A brief description of one <u>personal</u> <u>management</u> <u>activity</u> relating to Chapter 5. The activity could include the normal approach you implement in dealing with a sibling.

3.   A brief description of one <u>managerial</u> <u>incident</u> you have encountered <u>at work</u> as it relates to Chapter 5. This incident may include a description of the ethical code of conduct of your current employer.

4.   Reflections on the interrelationship of the class discussions and the out-of-class activity and incident you have recorded in 2 and 3.

In this way, you will be reporting on and verifying to what degree what you have read in the text and experienced in the classroom matches the reality of your daily personal and business life.

Your goals will be to better understand how managers really get things done through planning, organizing, leading, and controlling resources and by interacting with the firm's outside environment.

Also, this journal will serve as a means of developing your own critical thinking ability as well as your writing skill.

1.   Summary of Class Discussion

_____

_____

_____

_____

_____

_____

_____

_____

_____

_____

_____

_____

_____

_____

_____

_____

2. Personal Management Activity

Activity 1 _____

_____

_____

_____

Description 1 _____

_____

_____

_____

3. Managerial Incident Encountered

Incident 1 _____

_____

_____

_____

Description 1 _____

_____

_____

_____

4.   Reflections on Class Discussion as Related to:

Activity 1 _____

_____

_____

_____

_____

_____

_____

_____

Incident 1 _____

_____

_____

_____

_____

_____

_____

Chapter 5 Answer Key

Matching

Question	Answer	Question	Answer
1	b	11	d
2	k	12	m
3	t	13	h
4	a	14	n
5	i	15	e
6	p	16	s
7	f	17	g
8	r	18	o
9	c	19	j
10	q	20	l

Multiple Choice

Question	Answer	Question	Answer
1	a	9	b
2	c	10	d
3	b	11	c
4	d	12	b
5	c	13	a
6	c	14	c
7	b	15	d
8	a		

CHAPTER 6—THE ENVIRONMENT OF ENTREPRENEURSHIP AND SMALL-BUSINESS MANAGEMENT

Chapter Outline	Corresponding Learning Objectives
I. What Is Entrepreneurship? ● Entrepreneurship as an Option	LO. 1 Describe the importance of entrepreneurship to the U.S. economy.

II. Entrepreneurship and the Environment
  ● Definition of Small Business
  ● Impact of Entrepreneurial Companies	

III. Who Are Entrepreneurs?	L.O. 2 Define personality characteristics of a typical entrepreneur.

IV. Starting an Entrepreneurial Firm
  ● New-Business Idea
  ● The Business Plan
  ● Legal Form
  ● Financial Resources
  ● Tactics
  ● Getting Help
	L.O. 3 Describe the planning necessary to undertake a new business venture.
	
	L.O. 4 Discuss decision tactics and sources of help that increase chances for new business success.

V. Managing a Growing Business
  ● Stages of Growth
  ● Planning
  ● Organizing
  ● Leading
  ● Controlling
  ● Coping with Chaotic Times
	L.O. 5 Describe the five stages of growth for an entrepreneurial company.
	
	L.O. 6 Explain how the management functions of planning, organizing, leading, and controlling apply to a growing entrepreneurial company.

VI. Intrapreneurship in a Growing Business	L.O. 7 Discuss how to facilitate intrapreneurship in established organizations.

Major Concepts

(1) Our changing economic environment is both contributing to and benefiting from those people who have entrepreneurial and intrapreneurial characteristics. (2) Those entrepreneurs with such characteristics who also thoughtfully get their business off to a good start and use four management skills to guide it properly through its stages of growth have the greatest chance of success.

In your own words, *what did the above paragraph say?*   Perhaps the following will help you translate the above and strengthen your understanding of the sixth chapter!

First Sentence: The Entrepreneurial Impact
Until very recently, it was often very difficult for small businesses to survive in a business world dominated by large corporations. Business opportunity often involved the manufacture of tangible products, and the production involved very large investments for equipment and facilities. It took money to make money. You needed to be born rich if you wanted to go into business for yourself. Things have not totally changed, but they are changing.

Those still in the production of goods are forced to cut costs due to global competition. One way they have done that is to outsource activities to smaller entrepreneurs who can perform tasks at a lower cost. The manufacturers then downsize those aspects of their operations that have been outsourced. The downsizing has created a pool of potential entrepreneurs, and the outsourcing has created a demand for their services.

Furthermore, some employees who were once part of larger companies left voluntarily (not because of downsizing) because they recognized their own creativity and that they did not need the resources of a larger company to make effective use of their own talents. In today's world, intellectual capital—creativity and ideas—is often more important than financial capital. Having more money does not necessarily mean that you will have more creativity, but having more creativity may help you obtain more money.

That is partly due to the fact that our economy now has a greater focus on the production of services than goods. Many services are also subject to global competition. However, it requires vastly less investment to enter and be a low-cost firm in a service business such as hair styling or financial consulting than industries such as automobiles or steel. Unlike the advantage that a big manufacturer may have over a smaller manufacturer, a big service firm does not always have a significant advantage over a smaller firm, especially if the smaller firm is blessed with intellectual capital or creativity.

Larger companies have attempted to stem the loss of talent and compete with smaller companies by encouraging "intrepreneurship"—opportunities to launch ideas and ventures that are part of the corporation so that talented people do not have to leave in order to apply their ideas.

Personal characteristics that are common to such creative entrepreneurs/intrapreneurs include an internal locus of control (a self-disciplined self-starter), high energy level, need to achieve, tolerance for ambiguity (tolerance is not the same thing as preference), awareness of passing time, and self-confidence.

Second Sentence: Starting and Growing, Using Management Skills

Starting a business involves taking a creative idea and converting it into an organization. That requires a legal structure, a business plan, the necessary financial resources, and a means of management.

Selection of a legal structure, such as a proprietorship or certain forms of corporations and partnerships, will be affected by such considerations as taxes, the ease of starting, the need for additional resources, and the risk of lawsuits.   Preparing the business plan helps the entrepreneur to systematically think through and carefully spell out just what he or she is trying to do, how it is to be done, and who it will be done for. It helps the entrepreneur identify where he or she is headed and how to get there. It helps determine who is the customer and what exactly the customer really wants. It also covers the financial resources needed and the legal structure to be used.   Initial financing decisions include the amount of money to be put up by the owner or owners versus the amount to be borrowed. The amount of money initially needed may sometimes be reduced if the venture can operate within shared facilities such as a business incubator.   The incubator may also help provide management advice.

It is not always necessary to start from scratch and perhaps spend a lot of money to become well known and spend several years to become profitable.   Alternatives include buying out an existing firm that is already well-known, profitable, and has trained employees and loyal customers. One may buy out an existing independent firm or existing franchise.

One may also start up as a franchisee and have the benefit of a well-known name and the backing of a larger organization.

Many small businesses go through certain stages of growth such as being brought into existence, achieving the ability to survive, attaining success, really taking off, and then maturing. As the growth occurs, there will be special challenges in carrying out each function of management: planning, organizing, controlling, and leading.

Key Term Identification/Application

Matching Questions

Match each statement or situation with the key term that best describes it. (Note: Some terms may be used more than once.)

a. entrepreneurship
b. entrepreneur
c. internal locus of control
d. external locus of control
e. need to achieve
f. tolerance for ambiguity
g. business plan
h. proprietorship
i. partnership

j. corporation
k. debt financing
l. equity financing
m. venture-capital firm
n. franchising
o. business incubator
p. spin-off
q. intrapreneurship

_____ 1.   I have decided to use my personal assets as collateral and borrow $100,000 from the bank in order to start my business.

_____ 2.   The process of initiating a business venture, organizing the necessary resources, and assuming the risks and rewards.

_____ 3.   It is often necessary for a large, established company to recognize the need for innovation and promote it from within.

_____ 4.   I believe that my future or destiny is within my own control and that as long as I believe that, external forces will have little influence.

_____ 5.   Several of my best friends get together and invest money in new or expanding businesses because of potential future profits.

_____ 6.   Often students display their motivation to excel and pick situations in which they are likely to succeed.

_____ 7.   Several communities have facilities in which entrepreneurs are offered shared office space, management support services, and management advice.

_____ 8.   It is very important for any entrepreneur to prepare the document that specifies the details of the business prior to opening the new business.

_____ 9.   Sometimes the business owner decides that the best way to acquire the necessary funds to start and operate a business is to issue and sell stock.

_____ 10.   I own my own unincorporated business.

_____ 11.   This organization produces a product that is very similar to the product produced by our founder's previous employer.

_____ 12.   An artificial entity that has been created by the state and which exists apart and separate from its owners.

_____ 13.   Someone who recognizes a viable idea for a business product or service and carries it out.

_____ 14.   A less risky method of getting into business is the arrangement by which the owner of a product or service allows others to purchase the right to distribute the product or service.

_____ 15.   We often encounter people who believe that their future is not within their control but is largely influenced by external forces.

_____ 16.   Does it bother you not to known from where or when your next pay check is coming? Does uncertainty and disorder bother you?

_____ 17.   Two or more people often decide to formulate an unincorporated business and to act as co-owners of the business.

_____ 18.   McDonald's often allows people to purchase the right to distribute their products within a fairly tight set of standards.

_____ 19.   I think that I am an intelligent person with several strong skills and abilities that allow me to control my own future and that external events will have little lasting effect on me.

_____ 20.   William is in the process of starting his own painting business. He has gathered and organized the necessary resources and is ready to assume the associated risks.

Multiple-Choice Questions

Consider the following situations and, utilizing the appropriate management concepts, answer the multiple-choice questions that follow.

Situation #1

Your region of the country has the reputation of cleanliness and lack of pollution. It has also been blessed with an adequate abundance of natural resources and natural beauty, the least of which is not its crystal-clear streams and lakes. After a trip to another region of the country where you were amazed and disgusted with the poor quality and taste of the water, you are now considering entering the bottled-water industry.

1.   After talking with your brother about the idea, you are more than a little concerned. Your brother's view is that the world is a highly uncertain place, that anything could happen to affect the business, and that it is difficult to make things come out as desired. Based upon this discussion, you conclude that your brother:

   a.   has a strong internal locus of control.
   b.   has a strong tolerance for ambiguity.
   c.   has a strong external locus of control.
   d.   would make an ideal entrepreneur.

2.   You believe that you can make the difference between success and failure and that the future is within your control. You:

   a.   have a strong internal locus of control.
   b.   have a weak tolerance for ambiguity.
   c.   have a strong external locus of control.
   d.   should never go into business.

3.   People that know you would describe you as a high-energy person with a large amount of self-confidence. You also are motivated to excel and succeed but pick goals that are challenging yet attainable and that will give you a good sense of feedback about your success. You:

   a.   have a low achievement need.
   b.   have a high achievement need.
   c.   have a low tolerance for ambiguity.
   d.   none of the above.

4.   As you face the prospect of starting a business, you realize that it will be very challenging, time-consuming, and full of uncertainty. This is fine, for you do not need or like work situations that are clearly structured, have specific instructions, or provide complete information. You:

   a.   have a low achievement need.
   b.   have an external locus of control.
   c.   have a low tolerance for ambiguity.
   d.   have a high tolerance for ambiguity.

5.   After a considerable amount of self-study, you feel that you have the attributes that are required of an entrepreneur. You feel that providing quality bottled water at a moderate price in large urban markets is a good business idea, but you realize that you probably need to do more planning. A good business plan should include all of the following EXCEPT:

   a.   information about the industry, market, and suppliers.
   b.   financial information identifying the sources and uses of start-up and operating funds.
   c.   the business's policy for extending credit to customers.
   d.   the business plan should include all of the above.

6.   One of your initial key decisions concerning your business is the form of business ownership. If you choose the form that makes up 70 percent of all the businesses in the United States because it is so easy to start and gives you total ownership and control of the business, you are choosing a(an):

   a.   proprietorship.
   b.   partnership.
   c.   corporation.
   d.   franchise.

7.   Although you originated the business idea and have a good sense of the marketing requirements for your business, you know that you are very weak in the financial, accounting, and tax portion of the business. One of your best friends is very strong in these areas, so you are considering forming the business as co-ownership. You are considering forming a:

   a.   proprietorship.
   b.   partnership.
   c.   corporation.
   d.   franchise.

8.   Two of your concerns as you continue to mull over forms of business ownership are continuity of the business, if something should happen to you, and limiting your liability and not allowing a lawsuit to pursue your personal assets. The form of business ownership that would best address these concerns is:

   a.   partnership.
   b.   corporation.
   c.   franchise.
   d.   proprietorship.

9.   After choosing the corporation as the form of business ownership that best fits your circumstances and concerns, and before turning to the issue of raising the required capital for the business, you realize that your are acting as a(an):

   a.   intrapreneur.
   b.   business incubator.
   c.   entrepreneur.
   d.   none of the above.

10.   Because you have a significant amount of personal assets to show as collateral and fear losing control of the business, you are strongly considering obtaining a bank loan in order to raise required capital, or even selling corporate bonds. Both of these choices can be labeled:

   a.   equity financing.
   b.   venture capital.
   c.   small-business loans.
   d.   debt financing.

11.   While formulating your business plan, it becomes clear that you will need a sizable amount of capital to not only start the business but also to see it through the first 18 months of operation. This concerns you as you do not want to start operations with a large amount of debt on your books, which will eat up most of your profits. Perhaps it would be beneficial to consider the form of financing that would not requirement repayment. This form is called:

   a.   venture capital.
   b.   debt financing.
   c.   equity financing.
   d.   small-business loans.

12.   Recently you were contacted by three people who indicated that they would not only finance your business for two years, but they would also provide you with valuable business advice without expensive consulting fees. In return they would receive 50 percent of the profits over the first five years of operation. This form of financing is called:

     a.   venture capital.
     b.   debt financing.
     c.   equity financing.
     d.   small-business loans.

13.   The more that you investigate your business idea in the preparation of your business plan, the more risky and complex the business environment seems. Perhaps you should simply contact one of the established pure bottled-water distributors with their established distribution networks and see if you can purchase the rights to distribute their product. This form of business arrangement is called:

     a.   a corporation.
     b.   a partnership.
     c.   franchising.
     d.   a spin-off.

14.   Upon further reflection, you have decided that simply producing or distributing someone else's product or service is not what you had in mind when your business idea originated. One of your business contacts has notified you of a situation, sponsored by a government agency, that provides shared office space, management support services, and management advice to entrepreneurs like yourself. This innovation is called a(an):

     a.   spin-off.
     b.   business incubator.
     c.   business incinerator.
     d.   venture-capital firm.

15.   After all of the research, alternative evaluation, and decision making required in order to start a business with a good chance to succeed, you are dedicated to ensuring that your organization does   not chase away its most innovative people.   Therefore, you have established a process of not only recognizing the need for change but also of promoting it from within your organization. Your organization is promoting:

     a.   intrapreneurship.
     b.   entrepreneurship.
     c.   venture-capital firms.
     d.   spin-off companies.

Skill Practice Exercises

Just-Suppose Scenarios

Scenario #1

Just suppose that after graduating from college you obtained a job in an industry that you enjoyed, but with a company that, for whatever reason, did not match your personality or your career objectives. You are NOW considering starting a business of your own.

1.   Honestly assess yourself in terms of locus of control. What conclusions can you draw from this?

2.   How strong is your need to achieve and excel? Why do you think that?

3.   Do you have a high or low tolerance for ambiguity? What is the evidence to support this conclusion?

4.   Are you a good entrepreneurial candidate?

Scenario #2

Just suppose that you have decided that you are a good entrepreneurial candidate. What type of business would you like to open?

1.   For the type of business that you have identified, and given your own situation, what is the best form of business ownership? Why?

2.   Evaluate each of the following forms of business ownership as they apply to you and your business idea:

   Proprietorship

   Partnership

   Corporation

3.   How will you finance your business? Evaluate both debt and equity financing and determine the most appropriate form of financing for your business and your situation.

Scenario #3

Just suppose that upon consideration and evaluation, you have determined that you would not make a good entrepreneur because you need structure, need to know where and when you will receive your next paycheck, and, in general, have a low tolerance for ambiguity.

1.   You are still determined to go into business but have decided that starting a new business from scratch is not for you. Evaluate each of the following tactics and determine which is most appropriate for you:

A.   Buy an existing business

B.   Buy a franchise

C.   Participate in a business incubator

D.   Become a spin-off

2.   What conclusions can you draw from Scenarios 1, 2, and 3?

Personal Learning Experience

Interview

Contact the owner of a local business (not a chain store). The type of business does not matter. Ask the owner for an interview for this school project.

1.   Why did the owner go into business? How did the owner get into business?

2.   What form of business ownership is this business? From the owner's perspective, what are the advantages and disadvantages of this form of ownership?

3.   What advice would the owner give someone considering entering the industry and starting their own business?

4.   What conclusions can you draw from the above?

Integrated Case

Twenty-First Century Education

Jim Bowman was a member of the management staff at LDX TechnoSystems. However, he did not actually manage anyone. He was officially designated as a "Planner," but he often felt that he was really a "gopher" or general flunky.   Much of his time was not spent on routine planning but on non-routine projects and problems that did not seem to come under anyone else's jurisdiction. Nevertheless, Jim did not mind being a "general flunky" because it gave him an opportunity to become familiar with all areas of the business. Furthermore, he was often given wide latitude in carrying out his diverse assignments, so he was able to develop and exercise his creativity.

It occurred to Jim that LDX TechnoSystems was doing things that might enable it to become a partner with one or more universities. The partnership could be mutually beneficial to both LDX and the schools. For one thing, LDX provided high-tech training that very closely resembled the courses taught in some university computer science and engineering departments. Why not modify the courses so that they would qualify as the courses of an accredited institution or institutions and then enable the trainees at the LDX Training Center to accumulate college credits that could be applied to a degree at the partner university?   Also, in view of the fact that some LDX training was being provided to customers around the world using interactive multimedia through the Internet, why not offer those capabilities to universities so that they could offer their courses to a wide range of students around the world?

Jim bounced the idea off Jane Rand, the CEO, who then gave him a long list of reasons why it couldn't be done. However, he reminded her that he had long been accustomed to people at LDX telling him why something couldn't be done and then he would go ahead and do it anyway. She suggested that he talk to someone at his former alma mater and see what that person thought.

He talked to a former professor who was now a Dean. His former professor also had a long list of reasons why it was impossible. However, Jim pointed out that when he had been in school and belonged to various student organizations, the Dean had once observed that the impossible did not deter Jim from success.

Jim knew that his idea would not be easy to sell and would indeed be very difficult to develop and implement.   Although he tried to work on the idea as often as possible, he was being continually hit with a wide variety of other projects that left him with little time to develop what he thought could be a very useful and revolutionary use of LDX facilities. As a result, he finally went to Jane and suggested that he resign and become a consultant rather than an employee. He would work as the proprietor of his own business.

As a consultant, he would have access to the company facilities and could continue to use his former PC and other resources; thus, his need for start up funds would be nonexistent. He would be given one year to develop a proposed university venture for the company and would be given a share of its profits if it was accepted and implemented. If not, he would be given priority for reemployment if a position existed at that time—and he was informally assured that such would be the case. In many ways, his arrangement was similar to taking a leave of absence.

Case Questions

1.   Which entrepreneurial personality traits were demonstrated by Jim?

2.   Jim seems to have made certain decisions regarding the elements of a business plan. What are those elements and what were the decisions?

3.   What similarities does Jim have to a firm operating as a franchise? To a firm operating in a business incubator?

4.   Is Jim an entrepreneur, intrepreneur, or both? Why?

Journal Entries

Directions
The Study Guide will include a requirement that you keep a journal of your thoughts and actions relating to selected classroom discussions and corresponding chapter assignments from the text.

For selected class discussions and each chapter covered, you will log the following journal entries:

1. A summary description of Chapter 6 class discussions.

2. A brief description of one <u>personal</u> <u>management</u> <u>activity</u> relating to Chapter 6. The activity could include a comparison of a business plan with a personal growth plan for your own career.

3. A brief description of one <u>managerial</u> <u>incident</u> you have encountered <u>at work</u> as it relates to Chapter 6. This incident may include an example of intrapreneurship in your present or past work setting.

4. Reflections on the interrelationship of these discussions and the out-of-class activity and incident you have recorded in 2 and 3.

In this way, you will be reporting on and verifying to what degree what you have read in the text and experienced in the classroom matches the reality of your daily personal and business life.

Your goals will be to better understand how managers really get things done through planning, organizing, leading, and controlling resources and by interacting with the firm's outside environment.

Also, this journal will serve as a means of developing your own critical thinking ability as well as your writing skill.

1.   Summary of Class Discussion

_____

_____

_____

_____

_____

_____

_____

_____

_____

_____

_____

_____

_____

_____

_____

_____

2.   Personal Management Activity

Activity 1 _____

_____

_____

_____

Description 1 _____

_____

_____

_____

3.   Managerial Incident Encountered

Incident 1 _____

_____

_____

_____

Description 1 _____

_____

_____

_____

4.   Reflections on Class Discussion as Related to:

Activity 1 _____

_____

_____

_____

_____

_____

_____

_____

Incident 1 _____

_____

_____

_____

_____

_____

_____

_____

Chapter 6 Answer Key

Matching

Question	Answer	Question	Answer
1	k	11	p
2	a	12	j
3	q	13	b
4	c	14	n
5	m	15	d
6	e	16	f
7	o	17	h
8	g	18	n
9	l	19	c
10	h	20	a

Multiple Choice

Question	Answer	Question	Answer
1	c	9	c
2	a	10	d
3	b	11	c
4	d	12	a
5	d	13	c
6	a	14	b
7	b	15	a
8	b		

CHAPTER 7—ORGANIZATIONAL GOAL SETTING AND PLANNING

Chapter Outline	Corresponding Learning Objectives
I. Overview of Goals and Plans • The Importance of Goals and Plans	LO. 1 Define goals and plans and explain the relationship between them.
II. Goals in Organizations • Organizational Mission • Goals and Plans • Hierarchy of Goals	L.O. 2 Explain the concept of organizational mission and how it influences goal setting and planning. L.O. 3 Describe the types of goals an organization should have and why they resemble a hierarchy.
III. Criteria for Effective Goals • Goal Characteristics	L.O. 4 Define the characteristics of effective goals.
IV. Planning Types and Models • Management by Objectives • Single-Use and Standing Plans • Contingency Plans	L.O. 5 Describe the four essential steps in the MBO process. L.O. 6 Explain the difference between single-use plans and standing plans.
V. Planning Time Horizons • The New Paradigm	
VI. Thinking Strategically • What Is Strategic Management? • Purpose of Strategy • Strategy Formulation versus Implementation	L.O. 7 Define the components of strategic management.
VII. The Strategic Management Process • Situation Analysis • Business-Level Strategy • Porter's Competitive Forces and Strategies • Product Life Cycles	L.O. 8 Describe the strategic planning process and SWOT analysis. L.O. 9 Describe business-level strategies, including competitive strategies and product life cycles. L.O. 10 Enumerate the organizational dimensions used for implementing strategy.

Major Concepts

(1) In order for an organization to fulfill its mission through attainment of its strategic, tactical, and operational goals, it needs: strategic, tactical, and operational plans that are long-term, intermediate, or short-term; single-use, standing, and contingency plans; and management by objectives that undergo continuous improvement through a plan, do, check, and act cycle.
(2) The improvement of strategy begins with an analysis of the current mission, goals, and strategy and the current situation and then progresses to an overall strategy development, which ties competitive/business-level strategies together with the organization's product life cycle, recognizing the challenges involved in strategy implementation.

In your own words, *what did the above paragraph say?* Perhaps the following will help you translate the above and strengthen your understanding of the seventh chapter!

First Sentence: Mission and Goals, Plans and Planning

The organization's mission statement indicates its purpose for existence; its goals are intended to help it carry out that purpose. Plans are required to help the organization achieve its goals and thereby fulfill its reason for being.

Long-term goals require long-term plans, such as strategic plans, which may be five years in length. The achievement of overall long-term goals may be dependent on a variety of tactical goals for various organizational areas; thus, tactical plans, usually for an intermediate period of one or two years, need to be developed to achieve such goals. Operational goals are the specific, measurable results expected in the near future (such as during the next year) and thus require operational plans that are for that short term.

Some types of plans are for only a single-use such as a one-time project. Others are standing plans such as policies and procedures to handle situations that frequently occur. Contingency plans or "plan B" may need to be implemented if things do not work out as originally planned. Management by objectives is an approach that attempts to unite the entire organization through the planning process, with each person and department having measurable objectives that relate that person and department to the overall organizational goals.

Planning does not simply occur at one point in time and is then discontinued as the organization then implements the plan; instead, it requires continuous improvement to adapt the plan to new realities. The plan, do, check, and act approach is one such means of continually adapting the plan as needed.

Second Sentence: Strategy Development and Implementation

Since strategy is a plan that helps move the organization from where it is to where it wants to be, the first step is to determine exactly where it is now. What is our current mission, and what are the goals we have developed to fulfill that mission? What strategy do we now have in place to achieve those goals? Do our current mission, goals, and strategy make sense in view of our current situation? Analysis of the current situation involves a review of the organization's external opportunities and threats as well as its internal strengths and weaknesses.

With a clear idea of the current situation and any modifications concerning where it wants to go, the organization can develop growth, stability, and retrenchment strategies. The strategies can be specifically designed for each of its business units while simultaneously developing a comprehensive strategy that unites the entire organization. That strategy may be directed toward a market and involve a strategy of differentiation, cost leadership, or focus on regional market or buyer group. The strategy may be designed to offset the strategies of competitors who are going after that same market.

Again, strategy needs to be continually reviewed, especially in view of the fact that one's products will normally pass through different life cycles, and the strategy that is most appropriate to one stage in that cycle, such as introduction, may not be most appropriate for a different stage, such as maturity.

Brilliant strategy is of little value unless it can be implemented.   To the extent that the planning process, including strategic planning, involves not just top management but a large segment of the organization, it is likely that the strategy will therefore receive greater support and somewhat more enthusiastic implementation by those who have participated in its development than if it had simply been developed only by top management and then imposed on those who had no input.

Key Term Identification/Application

Matching Questions

Match each statement or situation with the key term that best describes it. (Note: Some terms will not be used.)

a.	goal	o.	Shewart cycle
b.	plan	p.	contingency plans
c.	planning	q.	strategic management
d.	mission	r.	strategy
e.	mission statement	s.	core competence
f.	strategic goals	t.	synergy
g.	strategic plans	u.	strategy formulation
h.	tactical goals	v.	strategy implementation
i.	tactical plans	w.	situation analysis
j.	operational goals	x.	differentiation
k.	operational plans	y.	cost leadership
l.	management by objectives	z.	focus
m.	single-use plans	aa.	product life cycle
n.	standing plans		

_____ 1.   It is very important to analyze the strengths, weaknesses, opportunities, and threats that will affect organizational performance.

_____ 2.   The organization's reason for existence.

_____ 3.   Even a small business needs to develop plans that define its response to specific situations such as emergencies or setbacks.

_____ 4.   Most of us are familiar with specific and measurable results that are expected from us as individuals or our work group.

_____ 5.   Our company has chosen a competitive strategy by which we are trying to distinguish our products from our competitors on the basis of durability.

_____ 6.   Our organization wants to increase its market share by 15 percent over the next five years.

_____ 7.   Plan, do, check, act.

_____ 8.   Most products will be introduced into the marketplace, experience growth, reach maturity, and then decline.

_____ 9.   Most budgets last for a year and then are reformulated.

_____ 10.   The act of determining organizational goals and the means of achieving them.

_____ 11.   We are going to concentrate on operational efficiency! Through cutting costs and establishing very tight cost-control procedures, we will become much more efficient than our competition.

_____ 12.   A desired future state that the organization attempts to achieve.

_____ 13.   The business activities that an organization does particularly well.

_____ 14.   The action steps by which an organization intends to achieve its strategic goals.

_____ 15.   Our organization allows managers and employees in every department to define goals that are in support of broader organizational goals and then uses those goals to monitor subsequent performance.

_____ 16.   In the very front of our college bulletin, we have a statement that broadly defines our basic scope and operations that will distinguish us from other organizations.

_____ 17.   Plans that are developed at the lowest level of the organization, which specify action steps for achieving operational goals.

_____ 18.   More and more organizations are concentrating their efforts on the aging baby boomers.

_____ 19.   The whole is greater than the sum of its parts acting alone.

_____ 20.   Policies are ongoing plans that provide us guidance for actions and tasks that are performed repeatedly.

Multiple-Choice Questions

Consider the following situations and, utilizing the appropriate management concepts, answer the multiple-choice questions that follow.

Situation #1

After determining that you have the skills, credentials, and patience necessary, you have decided to open an income-tax preparation service.

1.   Your business will offer extreme flexibility in terms of customer services offered. You will do whatever is convenient for the customer in terms of income-tax preparation. You will offer in-home or in-office "while-you-wait" service, or drop-off or mail-in service—whatever is most convenient for the customer. Your competitive strategy is that of:

    a. differentiation.
    b. cost leadership.
    c. focus.
    d. money.

2.   You have decided to concentrate your efforts on the income-tax needs of individuals and small businesses and will not target corporate or estate-tax preparation. This competitive strategy is that of:

    a.   differentiation.
    b.   cost leadership.
    c.   focus.
    d.   money.

3.   In order to formalize your thinking, you have prepared the following statement: "The purpose of Flex Tax is to provide extraordinary customer service in the preparation of individual and small-business taxes. Flexibility in meeting the income-tax preparation needs of our clients is our mission."   This statement is:

    a.   the company's strategic goal.
    b.   the mission statement of the company.
    c.   part of the Shewart cycle.
    d.   the tactical mission statement of the company.

4.   If you identify the action steps through which you will attain your broad organizational goals for the future, you are developing your:

    a.   strategic goals.
    b.   strategic management.
    c.   tactical plans.
    d.   strategic plans.

5.   An individual's goal to process 50 tax returns per day is which type of goal?

    a.   Strategic.
    b.   Tactical.
    c.   Operational.
    d.   Contingency.

6.   The organization's flexibility and dedication to superb customer service is the organization's:

    a.   synergy.
    b.   core competence.
    c.   strategy implementation.
    d.   single-use plan.

7.   It is important that an organization analyze its strengths, weaknesses, opportunities, and threats, not only in the beginning stages of operations, but periodically thereafter. This analysis can be identified as:

    a.   SWOT
    b.   SPOT
    c.   STOW
    d.   SOWT

8.   A very possible setback to your operation would be a series of tax audits by the Internal Revenue Service. It is important that the organization identify specific company responses to this possibility. These plans are called:

    a.   strategic plans.
    b.   operational plans.
    c.   tactical plans.
    d.   contingency plans.

9.   During the introduction to the marketplace stage and the growth stage of your service, which competitive strategy is most appropriate?

    a.   Differentiation.
    b.   Cost leadership.
    c.   Focus.
    d.   Efficiency seeking.

Situation #2

It is now five years later, and your operation has grown from one small four-person operation to an operation consisting of fifteen branch offices, with each branch office employing fifteen to twenty people.

10.   In a growing company it is important that all employees share and are committed to organizational goals. You have determined that the best way to ensure this is by using the managerial technique of having all managers and employees involved in the process of translating organizational goals into departmental and personal goals. These goals are then used to monitor and evaluate performance. This process is called:

    a.   strategic management.
    b.   contingency planning.
    c.   management by objectives.
    d.   the Shewart cycle.

11.   One of your organizational goals is to equip every employee of your growing company with the latest in laptop computers. Given the expense of the equipment, you have estimated that this might take two years to accomplish. This could best be described as a(an):

    a.   procedure.
    b.   policy.
    c.   rule.
    d.   program.

12.   Your organization is very committed to quality management and has instituted the Shewart cycle. Which of the following is NOT one of the elements of the Shewart (sometimes referred to as the PDCA) cycle?

    a.   Plan.
    b.   Develop.
    c.   Check.
    d.   Act.

13. We could label the organization's commitment to the Shewart cycle a:

    a. program.
    b. project.
    c. policy.
    d. procedure.

14. Everyone in your organization is well aware of your commitment to the planning process. An important part of the planning process is establishing effective goals. Which of the following is NOT a characteristic of an effective goal?

    a. Specific and measurable.
    b. Defined time period.
    c. Linked to rewards.
    d. Challenging to the point of being unattainable.

15. With a strong organizational commitment to management by objectives, it is important to understand the benefits and the problems with MBO. All of the following are benefits of MBO EXCEPT:

    a. the amount of paperwork.
    b. departmental and individual goals aligned with organizational goals.
    c. managers and employees communicating and focused on goal-oriented activities.
    d. the level of employee motivation.

Skill Practice Exercises

Just-Suppose Scenarios

Scenario #1

Just suppose that one of your strongest interests has always been music and that after graduating from college you have the opportunity to purchase an existing record store and go into business for yourself.

1.   Identify your mission and develop a mission statement for this business.

2.   Describe the relationship between goals and plans.

3.   Given your mission statement, develop your strategic goals and your strategic plans.

Scenario #2

Just suppose that as a college student you have been in the position (as a customer of the business) to observe the college from an operational viewpoint. Just suppose that you have been hired as a management consultant for the college after graduation.

1.   Identify the internal strengths and weaknesses of the college. Be specific!

2.   Now identify the external opportunities and threats for the college as we encounter the new millennium.

3.   Where in the product life cycle would you place the college? Why?

Scenario #3

Just suppose that you have completed the SWOT analysis for the college, as prescribed in Scenario # 2. It is now time to conduct effective strategic management.

1.   Which competitive strategy will be most effective for the college and why? How would you accomplish this strategy?

        Evaluate each of the following strategies:

        A.   Differentiation

        B.   Cost leadership

        C.   Focus

2.   What do you consider the core competence of the college? Why?

3.   What implication do the answers to questions 2 and 3 have for the college?

Personal Learning Experience

Research

Utilizing either the library or (preferably) the Internet, identify at least three articles on three different companies, either in the same industry or in different industries.

1.   From the information given, provide the mission statement of each company and give your interpretation of each one.

2.   What evidence of strategic management is evident? Support your answer.

3.   Identify the competitive strategies that each seems to be using.

4.   What conclusions can you draw?

Integrated Case

Participative Planning

When her chief planner quit to become an independent consultant, Jane Rand, CEO at LDX TechnoSystems, decided to not fill the position immediately but instead to temporarily assume all planning responsibilities herself and to review the organization's strategy.   She had an organization that was expanding globally into a wide variety of products, but she felt that it was doing so without any clear direction from anyone, including herself.

She decided to go back and rethink the company's mission statement—did it still apply, did the goals that had been previously selected still make sense?   She realized that she would need to revise strategy, but first, what was her situation?

She wanted to bring the entire organization into the planning process, and she decided to go about it quite differently. She knew that everyone was already busy simply trying to complete current assignments and did not have time to leave the tasks immediately at hand to do long-range strategic planning. To have the least disruptive effect on current output demands, she randomly selected a sample of both management and nonmanagement people who would work together. Management types would not have any greater voice than nonmanagement. Their job would be to brainstorm such matters as determining mission and goals. (Brainstorming involves letting everyone in the group submit ideas before any one idea is evaluated.) They would even analyze SWOT—Strengths, Weaknesses, Opportunities, and Threats. Then they would recommend a strategy of stability, growth, or retrenchment as they felt appropriate.

She pointed out that she held veto power and would indeed reject something or send back recommendations for further work if she felt that it was necessary. On the other hand, if they came up with recommendations that were not only accepted but which worked when implemented, they would receive a bonus and the success would be noted on each person's performance appraisal.

Case Questions

1.   Jane felt that the company may have strayed somewhat from its original mission statement and should therefore change the mission statement.   Another alternative might have been to go back to its original mission and eliminate things that deviate from it. What are the pros and cons of having a mission statement that remains fixed over the long run? What are the pros and cons of frequently modifying the mission statement?

2.   Jane is using a representative sample of management and nonmanagement people to brainstorm strategy so as to get the entire organization involved in the process and give people a feeling of involvement in something that will affect them. Evaluate the mixing of both management and nonmanagement people in the group, the use of only a sample, and the group approach to strategic analysis and development. Do you have any recommended changes? Why?

3.   Should Jane have submitted any suggestions or restrictions to her group of employees rather than giving them virtual free reign to submit their analysis and recommendation for her concurrence? What are the possible problems in reserving the right to veto what she doesn't like and sending it back to the group for further consideration?

4.   If Jane were to use the employee group to analyze and develop strategy, would it have been better if she had been part of that group? Why or why not?

Journal Entries

Directions
The Study Guide will include a requirement that you keep a journal of your thoughts and actions relating to selected classroom discussions and corresponding chapter assignments from the text.

For selected class discussions and each chapter covered, you will log the following journal entries:

1.   A summary description of Chapter 7 class discussions.

2.   A brief description of one <u>personal</u> <u>management</u> <u>activity</u> relating to Chapter 7. The activity could include a description of how goal setting has helped you in pursuing your college degree.

3.   A brief description of one <u>managerial</u> <u>incident</u> you have encountered <u>at work</u> as it relates to Chapter 7. This incident may include an example of the application of situational analysis to a strategic unit plan within your organization.

4.   Reflections on the interrelationship of these discussions and the out-of-class activity and incident you have recorded in 2 and 3.

In this way, you will be reporting on and verifying to what degree what you have read in the text and experienced in the classroom matches the reality of your daily personal and business life.

Your goals will be to better understand how managers really get things done through planning, organizing, leading, and controlling resources and by interacting with the firm's outside environment.

Also, this journal will serve as a means of developing your own critical thinking ability as well as your writing skill.

1.   Summary of Class Discussion

_____

_____

_____

_____

_____

_____

_____

_____

_____

_____

_____

_____

_____

_____

_____

_____

2.   Personal Management Activity

Activity 1 _____

_____

_____

_____

Description 1 _____

_____

_____

_____

3.   Managerial Incident Encountered

Incident 1 _____

_____

_____

_____

Description 1 _____

_____

_____

_____

4.   Reflections on Class Discussion as Related to:

Activity 1 _____

_____

_____

_____

_____

_____

_____

_____

_____

Incident 1 _____

_____

_____

_____

_____

_____

_____

_____

_____

Chapter 7 Answer Key

Matching

Question	Answer	Question	Answer
1	w	11	y
2	d	12	a
3	p	13	s
4	j	14	g
5	x	15	l
6	f	16	e
7	o	17	k
8	aa	18	z
9	m	19	t
10	c	20	n

Multiple Choice

Question	Answer	Question	Answer
1	a	9	a
2	c	10	c
3	b	11	d
4	d	12	b
5	c	13	c
6	b	14	d
7	a	15	a
8	d		

CHAPTER 8—MANAGERIAL DECISION MAKING AND INFORMATION TECHNOLOGY

Chapter Outline	Corresponding Learning Objectives
I. Types of Decisions and Problems • Programmed and Nonprogrammed Decisions	L.O. 1 Explain why decision making is an important component of good management.
II. Certainty, Risk, Uncertainty, and Ambiguity	L.O. 2 Explain the difference between programmed and nonprogrammed decisions and the decision characteristics of risk, uncertainty, and ambiguity.
III. Decision-Making Models	L.O. 3 Describe the classical and administrative models of decision making and their applications.

IV. Decision-Making Steps
   • Recognition of Decision Requirement
   • Diagnosis and Analysis of Causes
   • Development of Alternatives
   • Selection of Desired Alternative
   • Implementation of Chosen Alternative
   • Evaluation and Feedback
   • Decision Biases to Avoid
	L.O. 4 Identify the six steps of managerial decision making.

V. Increasing Participation in Decision Making
   • Vroom-Jago Model
   • Group Participation Formats
   • Advantages and Disadvantages of Participative Decision Making
	LO. 5 Discuss the advantages and disadvantages of participative decision making.

Chapter Outline	Corresponding Learning Objectives
VI. Improving Decision-Making Breadth and Creativity • Using Information Technology for Decision Making	
VII. Information Technology • Data versus Information • Characteristics of Useful Information	L.O. 6 Describe the importance of information technology for organizations and the attributes of quality information.
VIII. Types of Information Systems	L.O. 7 Identify different types of information systems.
XI. Strategic Use of Information Technology • Operational Efficiency and Control • Competitive Strategy	L.O. 8 Explain how information systems support daily operations and decision making for low-level management. L.O. 9 Explain how networks are transforming the way companies operate and the services they offer.

Major Concepts

(1) The programmed and nonprogrammed decisions that are made under conditions of certainty, risk, uncertainty, and ambiguity are not always made as they supposedly should be made using the classical model but may actually be made using the administrative model. (2) In pursuing the six steps of decision making, varying degrees of group participation may be used in one or more of the steps. (3) Information technology can help facilitate the decision-making process by transforming data into useful information in terms of time, content, and form through operational systems (for daily operations and low-level managers) and through management information systems for middle and upper management. (4) Decision making is also facilitated through other information systems that support a range of management levels and through technologies of groupware, geographic information systems, and networks.

In your own words, *what did the above paragraph say?*   Perhaps the following will help you translate the above and strengthen your understanding of the eighth chapter!

First Sentence: Decisions under Varied Conditions Using Different Models

Decisions involve identifying and responding to problems and opportunities. A decision may be programmed in the form of rules that apply to frequently recurring situations or it may be non-programmed because the situation is unique, poorly defined, and unstructured.

Decision conditions include certainty, which means the decision maker has all needed information; risk, which means that the goal and information are clear and adequate but outcomes are unclear; uncertainty, which means that the goal is clear but information and outcomes are unclear; and ambiguity, which means that everything is unclear: the goal or problem, the alternatives, and the outcomes.

The classical model assumes that decision makers make logical decisions in the organization's best interest using agreed upon goals and criteria with precisely defined problems. The administrative model assumes that managers often make nonprogrammed decisions under conditions of uncertainty and ambiguity and must use bounded rationality (the concept that there is only limited time and ability to make decisions) or satisficing (selecting the first choice that meets minimum criteria), building coalitions to support decisions, and using intuition.

Second Sentence: Use of Steps and Groups in Decision Making

The first step is to recognize the need for a decision because of a failure to achieve goals, known as a problem, or because of a potential to exceed goals, known as an opportunity.

The next step is very crucial. It involves diagnosing the cause or reason for the situation requiring a decision. Diagnosis must focus on the cause or causes, not just the symptoms. The subsequent steps include developing alternative solutions, selection of the best alternative, implementing the chosen alternative, and evaluation/feedback regarding the implementation.

Groups may be useful in decision making, because they may provide a broader perspective and an ability to evaluate more information and alternatives; the discussion may clarify issues; and the participation of members may result in greater support for the decision. However, groups may also result in wasted time, undesirable compromises, group norms that stifle dissent, and lack of responsibility for decisions. The Vroom-Yago model helps managers to determine the amount of subordinate participation in decision making by evaluating the leader participation styles, using diagnostic questions, and decision rules. Groups may be face-to-face such as "interactive," with specific agenda and goals and "nominal," which is structured to ensure that all have equal input. "Delphi" is a non-face-to-face group of experts whose ideas are gathered, shared, recirculated, and refined until a consensus is obtained. Other employee participation techniques include devil's advocate (someone challenges the group's ideas), multiple advocacy (different and contrasting views are presented), and brainstorming—the encouragement of uncensored ideas from all before any one idea is examined.

Third Sentence: Information and Operational and Management Information Systems

Information technology can help facilitate the decision-making process by transforming data into useful information. Information is useful in terms of time if it is up-to-date and provided for the period needed as well as when it is needed. It is useful in its content if the information is accurate, relevant, and complete. It is useful when it is presented in a form that is clear, has exactly the level of detail needed but no more, and is presented in the narrative, numeric, or spatial form desired.

Operational systems such as office automation systems, transaction processing systems, and process control systems are used for daily operations by lower-level managers. Management information systems such as executive information systems, decision support systems, and information reporting systems are used by middle and upper management for tactical and strategic decisions.

Fourth Sentence: Other Information Systems and Technologies Such as Networks

Decision making is also facilitated through other information systems that support either operations or management applications and therefore may support a wide range of management levels. Examples include group decision support systems and artificial intelligence as used in expert systems. Emerging technologies include groupware such as electronic messaging or E-mail, and geographic information systems, which present information through maps. There are various integrated combinations of the above systems.

Networks tie people, computers, and organizations together through local-area networks or wide-area networks. Middleware helps make communication possible between different types of hardware and software globally.

Key Term Identification/Application

Matching Questions

Match each statement or situation with the key term that best describes it. (Note: Some terms will not be used.)

a.	decision	aa.	devil's advocate
b.	decision making	bb.	multiple advocacy
c.	programmed decision	cc.	brainstorming
d.	nonprogrammed decision	dd.	information technology
e.	certainty	ee.	data
f.	risk	ff.	information
g.	uncertainty	gg.	management information system (MIS)
h.	ambiguity		
i.	classical model	hh.	operations information system
j.	normative		
k.	administrative model	ii.	transaction processing system
l.	bounded rationality		
m.	satisfice	jj.	process control system
n.	descriptive	kk.	information reporting system
o.	intuition		
p.	coalition	ll.	decision support system
q.	problem	mm.	executive information system
r.	opportunity		
s.	diagnosis	nn.	group decision support system
t.	risk propensity		
u.	implementation	oo.	expert system (ES)
v.	Vroom-Jago model	pp.	groupware
w.	interactive group	qq.	geographic information system
x.	nominal group		
y.	Delphi group	rr.	network
z.	groupthink	ss.	cluster organization

_____ 1.   The approach to decision making that indicates how the decision maker should make decisions.

_____ 2.   A good way to promote freer and more creative thinking within a group is by encouraging group members to spontaneously generate solutions to a situation regardless of the likelihood of those solutions being workable.

_____ 3.   A computer-based interactive system that encourages and facilitates communication and decision making.

_____ 4.   The situation in which accomplishments have failed to meet goals.

_____ 5.   The term, or approach, used to describe how managers actually make decisions rather than how they should.

_____ 6.   Raw, unanalyzed, and unsummarized facts and figures.

_____ 7.   Most often managers are faced with situations in which they know what goals they want to achieve, but information about either the situation or the alternatives is unclear.

_____ 8.   Samuel has been assigned the group role of challenging the group's assumptions and statements.

_____ 9.   At our organization, we use a system in which individuals in different locations communicate with each other through E-mail and group decision support systems to make decisions and solve problems.

_____ 10.   Sometimes a decision is required in a situation that happens frequently and is very routine in nature.

_____ 11.   Any system that organizes information in the form of prescribed reports that managers utilize when making day-to-day decisions.

_____ 12.   Many managers tend to choose the first solution that minimally solves the problem and stop searching for the best, or optimal, solution.

_____ 13.   A decision-making technique that utilizes several advocates to present several points of view including minority and unpopular opinions.

_____ 14.   A computer system that monitors and controls ongoing physical production processes.

_____ 15.   The goals to be achieved are unclear, alternatives are difficult to determine, and information about the situation is unavailable.

_____ 16.   Often group members are so committed to the group that they do not express contrary opinions.

_____ 17.   A system that links together people and departments for the purpose of sharing information resources.

_____ 18.   The reality is that people have the ability and the time to only process so much information with regards to a decision situation.

_____ 19.   A company's computer-based information system that supports its day-to-day operations.

_____ 20.   A model that has been designed to help managers to determine to what degree subordinate involvement is appropriate in the decision-making process.

Multiple-Choice Questions

Consider the following situations and, utilizing the appropriate management concepts, answer the multiple-choice questions that follow.

Situation #1

As a college student, you must make the correct decisions with regard to choice of courses, major field of concentration, and your career.

1.   Every quarter or semester, you are faced with the decision of what courses to register for the following quarter or semester. One of your aids in this process is a plan of study. You are engaged in the process of making:

    a.   programmed decisions.
    b.   nonprogrammed decisions.
    c.   descriptive decisions.
    d.   normative decisions.

2.   You know that you want to graduate from college in four years with a degree that will enable you to obtain a "good" job, but you do not feel that you have all the information available about either the area of concentration itself or job prospects in that area. This decision is being made under conditions of:

    a.   certainty.
    b.   risk.
    c.   uncertainty.
    d.   ambiguity.

3.   Several of your friends have advised you to choose a field of concentration in a rational manner. They believe that the primary criterion for the decision should be which field is in your best economic interest. Your friends are advocating the:

    a.   administrative model.
    b.   classical model.
    c.   normative model.
    d.   descriptive model.

4.   The university that you are attending offers 84 different majors or areas of concentration. You know that you will probably only investigate three or four possibilities, because you don't have the time or ability to process all the information available for decision-making purposes. This decision will be based upon the principle of:

     a.   satisficing.
     b.   intuition.
     c.   coalition.
     d.   bounded rationality.

5.   Your goal when you entered college and began taking courses was to maintain at least a 3.7 GPA. After your first quarter, and a little too much social life, your GPA is 1.6. What you have is a(an):

     a.   opportunity.
     b.   condition of risk propensity.
     c.   normative decision.
     d.   problem

Situation #2

During your college years, you have been working at a nationally known retail store in order to earn some money. Because you are attending your college and are majoring in Business Management, you have been promoted to Assistant Manager of the Household Goods department, even though you are working part-time.

6.   Recently the organization has made it very clear in an all-manager meeting that the organization will demand and expect extraordinary levels of customer service in the future. While this message is very clear, as the direct supervisor of 17 employees, you are trying to decide the degree to which employees should be involved in determing and communicating the standards of customer service. According to Vroom-Jago, the appropriate style of decision making would be:

     a.   A1
     b.   Gll
     c.   Cll
     d   All

7.   Your task is to identify a new, "catchy" advertising slogan for the store. You have decided to include your employees in this creative process. A good interactive group method that promotes freer and more creative thinking is:

   a.   brainstorming.
   b.   the nominal group technique.
   c.   multiple advocacy.
   d.   ambiguity.

8.   You are well aware that you have a few employees who tend to be very dominant, and you want to ensure that every group member has equal input into the decision-making process. An appropriate choice for this situation is the:

   a.   brainstorming method.
   b.   nominal group method.
   c.   normative group method.
   d.   devil's advocate method.

9.   One of your largest challenges in this slumping economy is declining sales.   You have identified 5 major points of view on the subject and desire input from your employees as to which is the best choice. You have decided to appoint two employees to represent each viewpoint and develop a presentation promoting that viewpoint, regardless of their true personal feelings. This method is called:

   a.   groupthink.
   b.   the Delphi group technique.
   c.   multiple advocacy.
   d.   brainstorming.

10.   Even though your employees seem to enjoy being involved in the decision-making process, you are very aware that participative decision making is not appropriate for all situations. One problem with participative decision making occurs when the group is so cohesive that they are reluctant to disagree with each other or the leader of the group, and group norms reduce dissent and opinion diversity. This is called:

   a.   bounded rationality.
   b.   groupthink.
   c.   intuition.
   d.   the nominal group.

Situation #3

After four years of working as Assistant Manager for a large national retail chain and five years of working as the General Manager of a store, you have been promoted to District Manager. You are responsible for the operations of 10 stores, approximately $30 million annually in sales, and almost 2,500 employees.

11. As you sit at your desk on Monday morning looking over the weekend sales reports from your stores and attempting to identify specific trends, you realize that you are looking at:

   a. information.
   b. data.
   c. groupware
   d. none of the above.

12. If the report that you are perusing has been generated by a computer-based information system, and the system supports your company's day-to-day operations, then you are utilizing a(an):

   a. group decision support system (GDSS).
   b. decision support system (DSS).
   c. operations information system.
   d. executive information system (EIS).

13. One of the keys to your type of business is acquiring and utilizing sales information of "hot" items in a timely manner. In order for you to obtain this information, your company has installed a system that updates the company's inventory on a real-time basis as each item is sold at the register. This type of operations information system could best be described as a(an):

   a. geographic information system.
   b. expert system.
   c. process control system.
   d. transaction processing system.

14. In order for you and your ten managers to better communicate and make better purchasing and marketing decisions, you have installed an interactive computer-based system that is sometimes called a collaborative work system. Another term for this system is:

   a. a network.
   b. a group decision system.
   c. an executive information system.
   d. a transaction processing system.

15.   From the interactive computer-based system described in question 14, you have decided that it is a logical and necessary step to change the organizational form itself to a form in which key employees in different locations communicate with each other via E-mail and the group decision system to better problem solve. This type of organization is called a(an):

    a.   cluster organization.
    b.   conglomerate organization.
    c.   complex organization.
    d.   classical organization.

Skill Practice Exercises

Just-Suppose Scenarios

Scenario #1

Just suppose that you are the owner and manager of Magical Movers, a local and regional moving company. Part of your job includes the task of scheduling moves and ensuring that the company has the resources necessary to meet the demand.

1.   Describe and give examples of the following types of decisions that you will be making:

        Programmed

        Nonprogrammed

2.   In terms of the nonprogrammed decisions that you identified above, describe the situation in terms of certainty.

Scenario #2

Just suppose that you have established yourself in the business of dog grooming in your area. You have discovered that your chief competitor is having health and financial problems.

1.   In the terms identified in the text, what type of situation is this?

2.   Using this example, differentiate between the classical model of decision making and the administrative model.

3.   Using the above scenario, give examples of:

    a.   Bounded rationality

    b.   Satisficing

    c.   Intuition

Scenario #3

Just suppose that your college teacher assigns you and four other students a large class project and presentation that must be done in six weeks. Assume further that the teacher has chosen you to be the leader of the group.

1.   Using Vroom-Jago, what is the most appropriate position with respect to participative management?

2.   For this type of task, which is the most appropriate group method? Why?

3.   Which method do you feel is the most unappropriate method? Justify your answer.

Personal Learning Experience

Research

Using either your local library or the Internet (if you have access to it), identify at least three companies that rely heavily upon the computer, whether computer-based or computer interactive, in the management of information for decision purposes.

1.   Compare and contrast the three companies. What are the challenges that they have overcome through computer-aided decision making?   What are the disadvantages?

2.   Would you like to work for one of these companies? Why or why not?

3.   Do all decision-making methods fit all situations? Describe your anticipated career path. What conclusions can you draw?

Integrated Case

Group Decisions

Jane Rand tried a new approach to her strategic planning. It involved getting a sample of employees together to brainstorm and develop recommendations that would be sent to her for approval or then returned to the group for further brainstorming. Although the outcome of the process was potentially important to the company, Jane's involvement was very limited.

The group of employees developed recommendations that often involved more commitment on the part of top management than it did for them. They were given only the relevant information that they requested, but many did not know what to request to gain insight regarding the many issues that seemed ambiguous. Their strategies avoided the use of any downsizing as a means of cost cutting.

Although the brainstorming sessions were supposed to be conducted in a way that permitted everyone to participate before any idea was evaluated, a few domineering people with long-held hostility toward top management emerged and generally tended to pour cold water on any positive ideas presented. These people didn't tear the suggestions of others apart until after all ideas were submitted, but they would emit groans and loud laughs at the ideas that they disagreed with—and that included nearly all ideas submitted.

When the first report was submitted, Jane rejected the results almost totally and sent it back for modification. The subsequent session became even less productive, and the report was so negative in tone that Jane disbanded the group and decided she would develop a strategy on her own. She had management information systems that she felt gave her all that she needed to develop such a strategy.

Case Questions

1.   Review the Vroom-Jago model and then explain why the group failed to produce useful results for Jane.

2.   In regards to brainstorming, what was done right and what might have been done differently?

3.   What technique other than brainstorming might have produced better results? Why?

4.   Jane expects that her management information systems will give her all that she needs to develop an effective strategy. Defend her view. Attack her view.

Journal Entries

Directions

The Study Guide will include a requirement that you keep a journal of your thoughts from class discussions and corresponding chapter assignments as described below.

For class discussions and each chapter covered, you will log the following journal entries:

1. A summary description of Chapter 8 class discussions.

2. A brief description of one <u>personal</u> <u>management</u> <u>activity</u> relating to class discussion in Chapter 8. The activity could include a discussion of what data you would need to make an informed decision on picking a stock in which to invest.

3. A brief description of one <u>managerial</u> <u>incident</u> you have encountered <u>at work</u> as it relates to class discussion in Chapter 8. This incident may include an application of the decision-making steps to a specific problem you face in your work unit.

4. Reflections on the interrelationship of the class discussions and the out-of-class activity and incident you have recorded in 2 and 3.

In this way, you will be reporting on and verifying to what degree what you have read in the text and experienced in the classroom matches the reality of your daily personal and business life.

Your goals will be to better understand how managers really get things done through planning, organizing, leading, and controlling resources and by interacting with the firm's outside environment.

Also, this journal will serve as a means of developing your own critical thinking ability as well as your writing skill.

1.   Summary of Class Discussion

_____

_____

_____

_____

_____

_____

_____

_____

_____

_____

_____

_____

_____

_____

2.   Personal Management Activity

Activity 1 _____

_____

_____

_____

Description 1 _____

_____

_____

_____

3.   Managerial Incident Encountered

Incident 1 _____

_____

_____

_____

Description 1 _____

_____

_____

_____

4.   Reflections on Class Discussion as Related to:

Activity 1 _____

_____

_____

_____

_____

_____

_____

_____

_____

Incident 1 _____

_____

_____

_____

_____

_____

_____

Chapter 8 Answer Key

Matching

Question	Answer	Question	Answer
1	j	11	kk
2	cc	12	m
3	nn	13	bb
4	q	14	ii
5	n	15	h
6	ee	16	z
7	g	17	rr
8	aa	18	ll
9	ss	19	gg
10	c	20	v

Multiple Choice

Question	Answer	Question	Answer
1	a	9	c
2	c	10	b
3	b	11	a
4	d	12	c
5	d	13	d
6	c	14	b
7	a	15	a
8	b		

CHAPTER 9—STRUCTURE AND FUNDAMENTALS OF ORGANIZING

Chapter Outline	Corresponding Learning Objectives
I. Factors Affecting Structure • Contingency Factor: Stages of Maturity • Contingency Factor: Manufacturing and Service Technologies • Contingency Factor: The Environment	L.O. 1 Describe how structure can be used to achieve an organization's strategic goals. L.O. 2 Describe four stages of the organizational life cycle and explain how size and life cycle influence the correct structure.
II. Organizing the Vertical Structure • Work Specialization • Chain of Command • Authority, Responsibility, and Delegation • Span of Management • Centralization and Decentralization • Coordination • Reengineering • Task Forces and Teams • Integrating Managers	L.O. 3 Explain the fundamental characteristics of organizing, including such concepts as work specialization, chain of command, line and staff, and task forces. L.O. 4 Explain when specific structural characteristics such as centralization, span of management, and formalization should be used within organizations.
III. Departmentalization • Functional Approach • Divisional Approach • Matrix Approach • Team Approach • Network Approach	L.O. 5 Compare the functional approach to structure with the divisional approach. L.O. 6 Explain the matrix approach to structure and its application to both domestic and international organizations. L.O. 7 Explain the contemporary team and network structures and why they are being adopted by organizations.

Major Concepts

(1) The use of an organic versus mechanistic design and the use of vertical structure in the overall organization and its departments depend on three contingency factors: size and stage of growth, manufacturing or service technologies used, and environmental certainty or uncertainty. (2) A vertical structure is a centralized or decentralized hierarchal arrangement of work specialization (jobs) into a flat or tall span of management and chain of command with authority and responsibility distributed up and down the hierarchy. (3) The difference between functional, divisional, and matrix departmentalization approaches is that the functional organizes around inputs such as labor skills, the divisional organizes around outputs, and the matrix yields two bosses by combining the functional and divisional. (4) The use of cross-functional or permanent teams for better coordination and the use of networks are two variations in departmentalization.

In your own words, *what did the above paragraph say?* Perhaps the following will help you translate the above and strengthen your understanding of the ninth chapter!

First Sentence: Organic or Mechanistic and Three Contingency Factors
Organic organizations are loosely structured and rely on lateral coordination, whereas mechanistic organizations are tightly controlled and rely on vertical structure. The use of an organic (versus mechanistic design and vertical structure) in the overall organization and its departments depends on three contingency factors: size and stage of growth, manufacturing or service technology, and environmental certainty or uncertainty.

The size and stage of growth factor involves a shift from a loose structure early in the life of the organization to a more rigid vertical structure as it grows and matures. The manufacturing or service technology factor generally produces more mechanistic organizations in manufacturing and organic organizations in services, but there are exceptions. The factor of environmental certainty or uncertainty tends to result in mechanistic organizations being more prevalent under environmental certainty and organic organizations more commonly used under uncertainty.

Second Sentence: Vertical Structures, What They Do and What Affects the Hierarchy
An organizational structure combines various tasks into jobs that are assigned to people. Structure clarifies authority, responsibility, and other relationships among organizational members. Organizational power may be centralized among only a few or it may be decentralized and dispersed among many.

The vertical organization is one that has multiple levels of management, with each level having power over the level or levels below, and it concentrates authority and responsibility at the top. A relatively flat organization is one that has very few levels, and managers have a wider span of management; that is, each manager has a large number of employees reporting immediately to her or him. A relatively tall organization has many levels of management in the hierarchy, but managers at each level tend to have a smaller number of people reporting immediately to them.

It is important that authority and responsibility be balanced. It can be very frustrating to be responsible for something but not have the authority needed to carry out the responsibility. It can be very dangerous if a person has authority but is not held responsible for his or her misuse of the authority.

Third Sentence: Departmentalizing Functionally, Divisionally, and by Matrix

The difference between functional, divisional, and matrix departmentalization approaches is that the functional organizes around inputs such as labor skills, the divisional organizes around outputs, and the matrix yields two bosses by combining the functional and divisional.

It would be rational to organize functionally if there was a common set of skills that have multiple uses, and if those who have those skills work more effectively when part of a single entity. It would be rational to organize divisionally if there were a common set of outputs that require a multiple set of inputs, and if those diverse inputs work more effectively when part of a single entity.

A matrix structure may combine the best of both functional organizations, each of which contains specialized human expertise, and the divisional organization, which requires varied expertise. For some in the divisional organization, that may result in having two bosses.

For example, suppose there is a company with a consumer electronics division and a food products division.   Each division specializes in a type of output that requires many different kinds of expertise including help from the Human Resource Department. However, a supervisor in the food products division may be under pressure to complete a performance appraisal for submission to the Human Resources Department at the same time the same supervisor has been given production objectives from within food products' chain of command. As a result, the supervisor may feel that she or he has two bosses.

Fourth Sentence: Cross-functional or Permanent Teams and Networks

Much as a matrix structure brings together different skills to focus on output objectives, cross-functional team members (who remain part of various functional departments) come together to focus their capabilities on specific organizational needs. In some companies, the team approach to work becomes the basis for organizing its units, especially those who have shifted from a functional focus to a process focus. The use of networks—that is, the management of tasks assigned to other organizations, not to one's own employees—is a useful approach in many situations.   For example, achieving an objective for a customer may require managing activities involving its suppliers.

Key Term Identification/Application

Matching Questions

Match each statement or situation with the key term that best describes it. (Note: Some terms will not be used.)

a.	organizing	t.	accountability
b.	organization structure	u.	delegation
c.	organization chart	v.	span of management
d.	work specialization	w.	tall structure
e.	size	x.	flat structure
f.	organization life cycle	y.	centralization
g.	birth stage	z.	decentralization
h.	youth stage	aa.	departmentalization
i.	midlife stage	bb.	functional structure
j.	maturity stage	cc.	divisional structure
k.	technology	dd.	matrix approach
l.	small batch production	ee.	two-boss employee
m.	mass production	ff.	matrix boss
n.	continuous process production	gg.	top leader
o.	flexible manufacturing	hh.	cross-functional team
p.	service technology	ii.	permanent team
q.	chain of command	jj.	reengineering
r.	authority	kk.	network structure
s.	responsibility		

_____ 1.   Because I am the teacher, I have the formal and legitimate right to make decisions, issue directions, and allocate resources.

_____ 2.   Most employee manuals have a visual representation of the organization's structure.

_____ 3.   Sometimes in order to make a dramatic improvement in cost, quality, speed, and service, there has to be a radical redesign of the business processes.

_____ 4.   Joan has 23 employees who report directly to her.

_____ 5.   Our organization is only two years old and we are growing rapidly because we are meeting the needs of the marketplace.

_____ 6.   Our company makes spacesuits for NASA. NASA supplies us with the specifications and we only produce a few at a time.

_____ 7.   Many successful fast-food organizations place decision authority for changing the product near the top of the organization.

_____ 8.   Our company has a structure that places positions into departments based upon similar skills and expertise, such as the accounting department and the sales department.

_____ 9.   Every organization must determine the degree to which organizational tasks are subdivided into individual jobs.

_____ 10.   The unbroken line of authority that links all individuals in the organization and specifies who reports to whom.

_____ 11.   In industries that are rapidly changing, it makes sense to push decision-making authority as far down the organization and as close to the marketplace as possible.

_____ 12.   A group of employees assigned to different functional departments who meet as a team to resolve mutual problems.

_____ 13.   When you assign someone a task, they have the duty to perform that task.

_____ 14.   Sometimes employees must report to and be accountable to two different bosses at the same time.

_____ 15.   Our organization believes in broad spans of control and few hierarchical levels.

_____ 16.   General Motors is an example of an organization that has become exceedingly large and mechanistic.

_____ 17.   Our trouble-shooting team, which consists of members from each of the major functional departments of the organization, has been so successful that we have all been permanently assigned to the team.

_____ 18.   The basis upon which individuals are grouped into departments and departments into total organizations.

_____ 19.   Because our production process is nonstop, we utilize technology that involves mechanization of the entire work flow.

_____ 20.   The process that managers use to transfer the authority and responsibility for a task to a position below them on the hierarchy.

Multiple-Choice Questions

Consider the following situations and, utilizing the appropriate management concepts, answer the multiple-choice questions that follow.

Situation #1

Throughout your school years, it seemed as if you were addicted to video games. After graduation, you have decided to combine this fascination with your management degree and start a computer software development company with a specialization in games and other simulations. After considerable thought, you have decided to call your business New Dimensions.

1.   In the beginning, the company consists of you and two friends: one is an expert in accounting and the other is an expert in marketing. Your area of expertise is, of course, the technical area. Your company appears to be in which stage of the organizational life cycle?

    a.   Birth stage
    b.   Youth stage
    c.   Beginning stage
    d.   Elementary stage

2.   Initially you have decided to develop and market a handful of programs to sell to vendors and then to respond to specific customer demand. Your production process can best be described as:

    a.   flexible manufacturing.
    b.   continuous process production.
    c.   small batch production.
    d.   mass production.

3.   After a year of operation, you find that your business is growing rapidly as some of your programs catch on. This stage of the life cycle is the:

    a.   midlife stage.
    b.   birth stage.
    c.   maturity stage.
    d.   youth stage.

4.   As New Dimensions grows, you find that the organizational tasks need to be formalized. You are the president and your two friends are vice presidents in charge of their areas. You have had to hire a third person as vice president in charge of production and operations. Each vice president is free to hire and fire personnel within their areas. The organizational structure can best be described as:
   a.   divisional.
   b.   functional.
   c.   matrix.
   d.   network.

5.   Because the organization has grown to over 50 employees, and you feel it is important for all to understand the organizational structure, you have developed a visual representation of the structure. This representation is called a(an):
   a.   organizational structure.
   b.   organizational life cycle.
   c.   organizational depiction.
   d.   organizational chart.

6.   One of the purposes of the visual representation of the organization's structure was to show the unbroken line of authority that links all individuals and shows who reports to whom. This unbroken line is the:
   a. chain of command.
   b. span of control.
   c. organizational structure.
   d. span of management.

7.   Another reason to develop the visual representation of the organization's structure is so individuals can easily and quickly identify the formal and legitimate right of a manager to issue orders, make decisions, and allocate resources in their areas. This right is called:
   a.   accountability.
   b.   responsibility.
   c.   authority.
   d.   ability.

8.   For the first three years of operations, you insisted that the three founders of New Dimensions make all the decisions. This is called:
   a.   decentralization.
   b.   centralization.
   c.   delegation.
   d.   span of management.

9.   As time has progressed and the business has grown, it has become more and more difficult for the three founders to make all the decisions. The three of you have mutually decided to encourage the process of transferring authority, responsibility, and accountability to positions below. This transfer is called:

     a.   departmentalization.
     b.   centralization.
     c.   delegation.
     d.   imagination.

10.   The three founders of New Dimensions and the new Vice President of Operations and Production have all agreed that in a fast-moving and quickly changing industry such as computer software development, it is imperative to encourage employee empowerment. One way of doing this is by having a large number of employees report directly to one supervisor, knowing that the supervisor cannot micromanage each employee in this condition. The number of employees reporting to one manager is called the:

     a.   span of management.
     b.   chain of command.
     c.   central theory.
     d.   none of the above.

11.   With a large number of employees reporting to one manager and with relatively few hierarchical levels, the organization will probably have a:

     a.   tall structure.
     b.   flat structure.
     c.   no organizational structure.
     d.   matrix structure.

12.   One of your concerns with the current functional structure of New Dimensions is the tendency of employees in different departments to concentrate solely on the interests and concerns of that department to the exclusion of the interests and concerns of the organization. As a result, you have decided to assign a few individuals from each functional area permanently to groups with the responsibility of resolving mutual problems. These groups are called:

     a.   cross-functional teams.
     b.   departments.
     c.   committees.
     d.   permanent teams.

13.   Another method of adding flexibility to the organizational structure is to combine the functional structure with the divisional structure. This is called the:

    a.   maturity stage.
    b.   network structure.
    c.   matrix approach.
    d.   none of the above.

14.   You are also aware that as the organization grows, it tends to become more bureaucratic and mechanistic. In order to keep the organization flexible and responsive to the market, it might be necessary to have a wholesale, start-from-scratch, radical redesign of the business processes. This radical redesign is called:

    a.   reengineering.
    b.   organizing.
    c.   networking.
    d.   work specializing.

15.   Another organizational structure that should be considered before the organization grows very large is that non-critical functions of the business be "farmed" out to other companies and these functions be coordinated and brokered by a small, efficient headquarters. This approach is called the:

    a.   matrix approach.
    b.   network structure.
    c.   divisional structure.
    d.   functional structure.

Skill Practice Exercises

Just-Suppose Scenarios

Scenario #1

Just suppose that you are well-respected for your common sense and your business and management knowledge. One of your friends has approached you to act as a management consultant for her flower shop business.

1.   What advice would you give her concerning organizing and work specialization?

2.   How would you characterize her technology?

3.   What implications does the technology have on the organization?

Scenario #2

Just suppose that as you gain experience as a management consultant, your expertise and reputation increase. You have recently acquired as a client a large printing company that does business on a national basis.

1.   What factors would be important in considering the appropriate organizational structure?

2.   What factors are important in considering appropriate spans of management?

3.   For this company, what are the advantages and disadvantages of encouraging delegation?

Scenario #3

Just suppose that you have been fortunate enough to get in on the ground floor of a rapidly growing food-service business that intends to start franchising its operations next year. The public has been very positively responsive to the organization's product and format.

1.   Describe the advantages/disadvantages of a tall/flat organization. Which would you recommend? Why?

2.   What would you recommend concerning the centralization/decentralization issue?

3.   Identify a possible use for the matrix approach for this organization. Would you recommend the matrix approach? Why?

Personal Learning Experience

Application

All of us in one way or another are customers of various governmental services. We are often frustrated with the nature of those services because they are impersonal, less than efficient, and bureaucratic. Assume that you have been given the opportunity, power, authority, responsibility, and accountability to revise the nature of those services.

1.   How would you characterize the structure of most (if not all) governmental services?

2.   Given the size and complexity of government organization and the nature of the task, pick a specific government agency and briefly describe how you would restructure it.

3.   Would reengineering be required to accomplish your directions?

4.   Would the structure that you have recommended be able to deliver the governmental service in question better than the current structure?   Justify your answer.

Integrated Case

Reorganizing

LDX TechnoSystem's CEO, Jane Rand, believed that one of the biggest impediments to change and organizational renewal was her very mechanistic organizational hierarchy, which had been developed when LDX was part of AmCom, an old and large producer of telecommunications equipment. AmCom had reached a stage of maturity during a period of relative stability in the industry, long before computers and other massive changes revolutionized the industry. The vertical structure meant many layers of management. The centralization of decisions meant that any proposed change would have to work its way up past many potential vetoes before it could reach its final decision maker. Therefore, change was slow, but that was just fine. Stability and predictability in products, policies, and people were viewed as virtues by employees as well as customers.

On the other hand, there had long been some problems resulting from the type of organization LDX had inherited from AmCom. Lower level managers were held responsible for certain outcomes. However, if something unique occurred that required a new way of achieving that outcome, the manager would often not have the authority to act without concurrence from a manager who is at one or more higher levels. The concurrence would often be slow in arriving. By the time concurrence was obtained, there might be insufficient time to implement the change in order to achieve desired outcomes. Nevertheless, the manager would still be held responsible if he or she failed to produce the outcome.

Jane felt that the reason for AmCom having such a mechanistic system was that it was primarily in manufacturing. Furthermore, AmCom had produced a product that had not begun to change much until fairly recent times. On the other hand, she felt that such a system was not necessary for LDX, an organization that was primarily in training services. LDX needed to be able to quickly adapt to changing customer needs.

Many of the training programs LDX conducted for customers were actually jointly developed with the customers, conducted on customer premises, and included working with customers so that they could deliver training to their own employees without use of LDX trainers. Her organizational structure must be able to integrate itself into the structure of customers.

Case Questions

1.   Would you recommend that Jane implement a functional, divisional, or matrix structure? Why?

2.   What recommendation would you make to help bring authority and responsibility into balance?

3.   Jane feels it is crucial that LDX people become integrated into the organizations of customers that use LDX training.   How could your recommended organizational approach help achieve that objective?

4.   When LDX was part of AmCom, it was highly regarded for its predictability and stability. Now it needs to be able to rapidly change. Is there any way to organize the company so that it will provide customers with both predictability and responsiveness to change? How?

Journal Entries

Directions
The Study Guide will include a requirement that you keep a journal of your thoughts from class discussions and corresponding chapter assignments as described below.

For class discussions and each chapter covered, you will log the following journal entries:

1.   A summary description of Chapter 9 class discussions.

2.   A brief description of one <u>personal</u> <u>management</u> <u>activity</u> relating to class discussion in Chapter 9. The activity could include an explanation of the concepts of authority, responsibility, and delegation as they apply to your family unit.

3.   A brief description of one <u>managerial</u> <u>incident</u> you have encountered <u>at work</u> as it relates to class discussion in Chapter 9. This incident may include a description of how task forces and teams are utilized at your place of work.

4.   Reflections on the interrelationship of the class discussions and the out-of-class activity and incident you have recorded in 2 and 3.

In this way, you will be reporting on and verifying to what degree what you have read in the text and experienced in the classroom matches the reality of your daily personal and business life.

Your goals will be to better understand how managers really get things done through planning, organizing, leading, and controlling resources and by interacting with the firm's outside environment.

Also, this journal will serve as a means of developing your own critical thinking ability as well as your writing skill.

1.   Summary of Class Discussion

_____

_____

_____

_____

_____

_____

_____

_____

_____

_____

_____

_____

_____

_____

2.   Personal Management Activity

Activity 1 _____

_____

_____

_____

Description 1 _____

_____

_____

_____

3.   Managerial Incident Encountered

Incident 1 _____

_____

_____

_____

Description 1 _____

_____

_____

_____

4.   Reflections on Class Discussion as Related to:

Activity 1 _____

_____

_____

_____

_____

_____

_____

_____

Incident 1 _____

_____

_____

_____

_____

_____

_____

Chapter 9 Answer Key

Matching

Question	Answer	Question	Answer
1	r	11	z
2	c	12	hh
3	jj	13	s
4	v	14	ee
5	h	15	x
6	l	16	j
7	y	17	ii
8	bb	18	aa
9	d	19	n
10	q	20	u

Multiple Choice

Question	Answer	Question	Answer
1	a	9	c
2	c	10	a
3	d	11	b
4	b	12	d
5	a	13	c
6	c	14	a
7	d	15	b
8	b		

CHAPTER 10—INNOVATION AND CHANGE

Chapter Outline	Corresponding Learning Objectives
I. The Learning Organization	L.O. 1 Define organizational change and explain the forces for change.
II. Model of Planned Organizational Change • Forces for Change • Need for Change	L.O. 2 Describe the sequence of four change activities that must be performed in order for change to be successful.
III. Initiating Change • Search • Creativity • Idea Champions and New-Venture Teams	L.O. 3 Explain the techniques managers can use to facilitate the initiation of change in organizations, including idea champions and new-venture teams.
IV. Implementing Change • Resistance to Change • Force Field Analysis • Implementation Tactics	L.O. 4 Define sources of resistance to change. L.O. 5 Explain force field analysis and other implementation tactics that can be used to overcome resistance to change.
V. Types of Planned Change • Technology Changes • New-Product Changes • Structural Changes	L.O. 6 Explain the difference among technology, product, structure, and culture/people changes. L.O. 7 Explain the change process—bottom up, top down, horizontal—associated with each type of change.
VI. Culture/People Changes • Organizational Development	L.O. 8 Define organizational development and organizational revitalization.

193

Major Concepts

(1) The learning organization effectively uses the following four elements of change: first, the internal and external forces for change; second, the perceived need for change; third, the three means of change initiation: organizationally designed creativity, change agents, and new-venture teams; and fourth, the five means of change implementation: force field analysis, communication, participation, negotiation, coercion, and top management support.   (2) Types of change and the best approach for accomplishing the change include the following four: first, technology approached bottom up; second, new product approached horizontally; third, structure defined as hierarchy, goals, administrative procedures, and management systems and approached top down; and fourth, culture/people characterized by mergers and acquisitions, organizational decline/revitalization, and conflict management approached using the organizational development processes of unfreezing, changing, and refreezing.

In your own words, *what did the above paragraph say?*   Perhaps the following will help you translate the above and strengthen your understanding of the tenth chapter!

First Sentence: Change—Forces, Perceived Need, Initiation, and Implementation
The learning organization embraces continuous change. It effectively uses the four elements of change.   First, the forces for change may be internal, originating from those who are part of the organization, and they may be external, originating from competitors, the local community, and others who are not part of the company. Second, change is not only brought about or revisited due to the actual need, it is also affected by the extent to which people think that change is or is not needed. Third, change can be initiated by designing creativity into the organization through such means as open channels of communication, acceptance of mistakes, encouraging people to be change agents (champion new ideas), and forming new-venture teams whose very purpose is to produce change. Fourth, change can be implemented by the following six means: force field analysis (an analysis of the forces producing and resisting change); communication to facilitate understanding of the need for change; participation in the process of change by those who will be affected; negotiation to implement change in a way that will be most acceptable to those adversely affected; coercion in a crisis or other difficult situation; and top management support.

Second Sentence: Types of Change and Approaches to Change
Changes involving technology are best approached bottom up; that is, those technical specialists who know most about the technology should play a major role in decisions regarding its use.

New-product changes should be approached horizontally by people at the same functional levels such as marketing, production, finance, etc. Those in marketing may know better than others what the customer wants in the way of a product, but marketing must coordinate with production to determine whether it would be possible to provide what is desired by the customer at a price the customer is willing to pay. Marketing should coordinate with finance to determine what impact the product change will have on the firm's financial needs and resources.

Those at the top of the organization are assumed to have a better view of the so-called "big picture" and thus be best qualified to determine structural changes such as the hierarchy of authority, goals, administrative procedures, and management systems.

Changes in the organizational culture and the way people think and feel require special organizational development (OD) processes. The need for OD intervention may occur when culture clashes and morale problems accompany mergers and acquisitions. It may occur when the organizational decline is partially due to attitudes and the need for revitalization. It may occur as a result of the debilitating effects of organizational conflict and divisiveness. The OD approach involves beginning with diagnosis (unfreezing), intervention (changing through such means as team building or training), and refreezing—i.e., reinforcing the new attitudes and behavior.

Key Term Identification/Application

Matching Questions

Match each statement or situation with the key term that best describes it. (Note: Some terms will not be used.)

a.	organizational change	l.	horizontal linkage model
b.	learning organization	m.	time-based competition
c.	performance gap	n.	structural change
d.	search	o.	culture/people change
e.	creativity	p.	organizational development
f.	idea champion	q.	team building
g.	new-venture team	r.	survey feedback
h.	new-venture fund	s.	unfreezing
i.	force field analysis	t.	change agent
j.	technology change	u.	changing
k.	product change	v.	refreezing

_____ 1.   In today's world, it is important to encourage the development of new or novel solutions to organizational problems.

_____ 2.   One type of organizational development that increases departmental cohesiveness by helping employees learn how to function as a team.

_____ 3.   In order to be more competitive, we must deliver our products and services faster than our competition.

_____ 4.   Lois is an organizational development specialist whom we have hired to help us facilitate some needed changes.

_____ 5.   We know how difficult it is to encourage the development of new ideas while still producing the old products, so we have created an organizational unit that is separate from the organizational mainstream and which is responsible for initiating and developing innovations.

_____ 6.   A change in the output of an organization's products or services.

_____ 7.   The step in organizational development in which employees experiment with new workplace behavior.

_____ 8.   We are fortunate to have an organization in which everyone is engaged in the process of identifying and solving problems, which enables us to continuously improve.

_____ 9.   The most important changes often are stimulated by a person within the organization who sees the need for and champions a productive change.

_____ 10. The step in organizational development in which individuals who have acquired a new skill or attitude are rewarded or reinforced for doing so.

_____ 11. The adoption of a new idea or behavior by an organization.

_____ 12. As organizations grow, a change in the way the organization is designed, structured, or managed is often appropriate.

_____ 13. The approach to product change that emphasizes shared development of innovations among and between several departments.

_____ 14. Our college needs to learn about how other colleges are handling the financial aid process, since this is an area in which the organization needs to change.

_____ 15. Our organization needs to change the trust level between management and the employees.

_____ 16. In order to ensure that the change occurs and is accepted, it is imporant to initially analyze which forces, internal and external, support the change, and which forces resist the change.

_____ 17. One of the first things our change agent did after coming into our organization was to distribute questionnaires among the employees to obtain feedback on employee attitudes and satisfaction and then analyze the results.

_____ 18. It is important not only to encourage new ideas and innovations but also to provide resources to fund the development of the ideas and innovations.

_____ 19. The step of organizational development in which people are made aware of the problems that create a need for change.

_____ 20. There certainly is a difference, or disparity, between our desired performance levels and existing performance levels.

Multiple-Choice Questions

Consider the following situations and, utilizing the appropriate management concepts, answer the multiple-choice questions that follow.

Situation #1

After several years of teaching, you have been hired as a high school principal. You and your school must react, and sometimes change, in response to the needs of the teachers, the students, the community, the parents, and other schools.

1. The state average for students passing a high school proficiency test is 83%. Your passing rate is 61%. There is obviously a disparity between existing performance levels and desired performance levels. This is called the:

    a.   organizational mission.
    b.   performance gap.
    c.   new-venture.
    d.   organizational mandate.

2. In your staff meeting, you have strongly encouraged your teachers and staff to contact other high schools across the state to discover how and why their passing rate is so high, because your passing rate needs to change! You are encouraging them to participate in:

    a.   becoming change agents.
    b.   a new-venture team.
    c.   a search.
    d.   refreezing.

3. Even though some of your ideas concerning change are encountering widespread resistance, you are convinced of the need for change. You feel that you are championing productive change within the school. You are a(an):

    a.   idea champion.
    b.   implementor.
    c.   change agent.
    d.   advocate.

4. After reporting back from their search, the teachers and the staff have a variety of ideas and concepts that have worked to differing degrees at other schools. It is going to be impossible to implement them all, so you have appointed a six-person team that will be relieved of teaching duties and will be responsible for developing and initiating innovations for your school. This group is a:

   a. cross-functional team.
   b. quality circle.
   c. committee.
   d. new-venture team.

5. One of the most important steps to accomplish prior to changing policies and procedures at the school is to identify the forces, both internal and external, that are pushing or driving the change as well as the forces that are resisting the change. This process is called:

   a. monitoring.
   b. force field analysis.
   c. new-venture funding.
   d. unfreezing.

6. One of the changes that is being considered would entail changing from the traditional movement of students from class to class to a situation in which the students stay in one place with different teachers coming to them and attempting to teach curriculum in a unified and coherent manner. This change can be called a:

   a. horizontal linkage model.
   b. product change.
   c. time-based competition.
   d. structural change.

7. One of the problems that you have identified that needs to be changed is the attitude of the teachers and staff towards the school and the administration. This change would be a:

   a. culture/people change.
   b. structural change.
   c. technology change.
   d. product change.

8.   After identifying the need for change as well as some of the desired changes, you have contracted with an organizational development specialist outside the organization who will come in and facilitate the change. This person is the:

    a.   idea champion.
    b.   manipulator.
    c.   change agent.
    d.   mover.

9.   One of the first things that the change agent did when she arrived at your school was to distribute questionnaires to teachers, staff, and parents concerning the values, climate, participation, and group cohesion. After the survey was completed, she met with the various groups to give feedback about the responses. The change agent was utilizing the organizational development tool of:

    a.   team building.
    b.   survey feedback.
    c.   building horizontal linkages.
    d.   new-venture teams.

10.   One of the important concepts that has been discovered in the whole process is that the school as an organization is staffed by people who are engaged in identifying and solving problems. The school is a(an):

    a.   learning organization.
    b.   new-venture organization.
    c.   organizational development focus.
    d.   idea champion.

Scenario #2

You have just been notified by the president of the company that your company will be merging with a competitor in two months. At your urging, the president has agreed to delay the announcement of the merger for two weeks while you prepare your employees.

11.   This change can best be viewed as a:

    a.   technology change.
    b.   culture/people change.
    c.   structural change.
    d.   product change.

12. The first step of organizational development, and one that you must commence immediately, is the step in which employees are made aware of the problems that caused the change so as to increase their willingness to change. This first step is called:

    a.   team building.
    b.   changing.
    c.   refreezing.
    d.   unfreezing.

13. Your change agent has encouraged training employees to function as a team as a way of building cohesiveness between the members of the two formerly competitive companies. This technique is called:

    a.   team building.
    b.   survey feedback.
    c.   unfreezing.
    d.   culture/people change.

14. The second stage of organizational development is the step in which individuals experiment with new workplace behavior. This stage is called:

    a.   team building.
    b.   unfreezing.
    c.   changing.
    d.   refreezing.

15. The final stage of organizational development is the reinforcement of new employee skills and attitudes. This step is called:

    a.   team building.
    b.   refreezing.
    c.   unfreezing.
    d.   changing.

Skill Practice Exercises

Just-Suppose Scenarios

Scenario #1

Just suppose that you have always enjoyed being outdoors and working for yourself and therefore have started your own lawn-care and nursery business. Your flowers and shrubs are always of good quality and your business has grown. Recently though you have been hearing rumblings from some of your best customers that indicate that your operation is overpriced, takes too long, and doesn't use the latest technology.

1.   In terms discussed in the text, discuss your reaction to these challenges.

2.   Utilize force field analysis in analyzing the driving and resisting forces in this situation.

3.   Which type(s) of changes are necessary?

Scenario #2

Just suppose that your company is developing a new all-digital television that will make current televisions obsolete. Your company has a considerable stake in the success of this project. Many of your employees are skeptical and worried about this project and the future of the company.

1.   What type of change is this television?

2.   If you were the change agent, how would you handle the internal resisting forces?

3.   Describe the unfreezing, changing, refreezing sequence as it applies to your internal management of this change.

Scenario #3

Just suppose that you are the owner/manager of a small grocery store. You pay above-average wages, and you close every evening by 9:00 pm. You have recently discovered that a large grocery chain is opening a store in your town in six months.

1.   Identify the different types of changes that this situation indicates are necessary.

2.   Utilize force field analysis and determine the driving and resisting forces in this situation.

3.   Carefully and specifically explain how you will implement the changes that you have identified.

Personal Learning Experience

Interview

Make an appointment to talk with the customer-service manager at your local cable-television company.

1.   How does the organization identify in advance the need for change?

2.   What types of changes are the most common in this business?

3.   How does the organization manage change?

4.   Evaluate your interview.

Integrated Case

Changing the Boss

Ted Hanson sat outside the office of Jane Rand, CEO of LDX TechnoSystems.   He had an appointment to meet with her at 2:00 pm, but she was evidently running behind in her schedule. So, he simply sat in one of the very comfortable chairs in the waiting area and reflected on his challenge.

In his college business courses, the professors discussed change. However, with very few exceptions, change was discussed from the perspective of how managers can overcome their employees' resistance to change.   He was awaiting the meeting because his problem was just the opposite.

He had some ideas regarding how technology could facilitate telecommuting and possible outsourcing to overseas suppliers. His proposal could enable the company to sell its headquarters building and many of its other facilities and reduce labor costs through elimination of unneeded skills while simultaneously increasing compensation for those who would be vital in the new environment.

He wasn't surprised to find support from fellow employees who would benefit and opposition from those who would not. However, he was surprised at the almost universal opposition from all levels of management, even though most of them would not lose their jobs. There was a long list of reasons managers gave for opposing the change.

They pointed out that no other firm in the same business had applied what Ted was suggesting; therefore, it must not be a good idea. Many argued that the current system seemed to be working just fine, so "if it ain't broke, don't fix it."   Some pointed out that there may be a possibility of profits, but there is a certainty of costs, and they don't have the funds in the budget.   It was claimed that the idea may have merit, but this isn't the best time to be implementing it because there are higher priority issues to be dealt with at the present time.   There were those who said that the elimination of the facilities would destroy a community landmark.   Nearly everyone pointed out that the elimination of those who had long and faithfully served the company would destroy morale and ruin the company's public image.   The list went on and on.

It seemed obvious that LDX managers liked their facilities, enjoyed the social relationships they had developed within the organization, found the pace of work and the way work was done to be very pleasant, and had developed sentimental attachments to old equipment that brought back enjoyable memories. Some liked the current environment and organizational culture so much that they would put in more hours than were necessary. Some were delaying retirement because they didn't want to leave. What Ted was proposing seemed to destroy a cherished way of life. It seemed to be coldly and callously throwing the efforts of entire careers onto the scrap heap.

As he sat waiting to meet with Jane, he wondered if he could convince her of the benefits involved in his proposal. If he could, would she still be unwilling to go along with the proposal because of the opposition in the organization? What could he suggest that she do to overcome the opposition?

Case Questions

1.   Ted represents which element (or elements) of change? Which element (or elements) must be modified in order for Ted's proposed change to occur?

2.   Were you ever part of an organization (place of employment, club, church, etc.) in which you saw something that you thought should be changed?   What did you try to do in order to produce a change? What resistance did you meet? If you overcame the resistance, how did you do it?

3.   What suggests that Ted's proposal involves more than one major type of change? Since each type of change involves certain approaches that seem to work best, how should he approach change in a situation that combines types of change?

4.   Indicate specific actions you would use in applying OD as an approach to change at LDX.

Journal Entries

Directions
The Study Guide will include a requirement that you keep a journal of your thoughts from class discussions and corresponding chapter assignments as described below.

For class discussions and each chapter covered, you will log the following journal entries:

1.   A summary description of Chapter 10 class discussions.

2.   A brief description of one <u>personal</u> <u>management</u> <u>activity</u> relating to class discussion in Chapter 10. The activity could include a description of how you would use force field analysis to institute a change in your life.

3.   A brief description of one <u>managerial</u> <u>incident</u> you have encountered <u>at work</u> as it relates to class discussion in Chapter 10. This incident may include an explanation of how a structural change could aid your company or department in achieving higher productivity.

4.   Reflections on the interrelationship of the class discussions and the out-of-class activity and incident you have recorded in 2 and 3.

In this way, you will be reporting on and verifying to what degree what you have read in the text and experienced in the classroom matches the reality of your daily personal and business life.

Your goals will be to better understand how managers really get things done through planning, organizing, leading, and controlling resources and by interacting with the firm's outside environment.

Also, this journal will serve as a means of developing your own critical thinking ability as well as your writing skill.

1.   Summary of Class Discussion

---

2.   Personal Management Activity

Activity 1 _____

_____

_____

_____

Description 1 _____

_____

_____

_____

3.   Managerial Incident Encountered

Incident 1 _____

_____

_____

_____

Description 1 _____

_____

_____

_____

4.   Reflections on Class Discussion as Related to:

Activity 1 _____

_____

_____

_____

_____

_____

_____

_____

_____

Incident 1 _____

_____

_____

_____

_____

_____

_____

_____

Chapter 10 Answer Key

Matching

Question	Answer	Question	Answer
1	e	11	a
2	q	12	n
3	m	13	l
4	t	14	d
5	g	15	o
6	k	16	i
7	u	17	r
8	b	18	h
9	f	19	s
10	v	20	c

Multiple Choice

Question	Answer	Question	Answer
1	b	9	b
2	c	10	a
3	a	11	c
4	d	12	d
5	b	13	a
6	d	14	c
7	a	15	b
8	c		

CHAPTER 11—HUMAN RESOURCE MANAGEMENT

Chapter Outline	Corresponding Learning Objectives
I. Strategic Goals of HRM	L.O. 1 Explain the role of human resource management in organizational strategic planning.
II. Environmental Influences on HRM • Competitive Strategy • Federal Legislation • Trends in Society	L.O. 2 Describe federal legislation and societal trends that influence human resource management.
III. Attracting an Effective Workforce • Human Resource Planning • Recruiting • Selecting	L.O. 3 Describe how human resource professionals work with line managers to attract, develop, and maintain human resources in the organization.
	L.O. 4 Explain how organizations determine their future staffing needs through human resource planning.
	L.O. 5 Describe the tools managers use to recruit and select employees.
IV. Developing an Effective Workforce • Training and Development • Performance Appraisal	L.O. 6 Describe how organizations develop an effective workforce through training and performance appraisal.
V. Maintaining an Effective Workforce • Compensation • Wage and Salary Structure • Benefits • Termination	L.O. 7 Explain how organizations maintain a workforce through the administration of wages and salaries, benefits, and terminations.

Major Concepts

(1) The human resource department supports the overall organization by contributing to competitive strategies ranging from downsizing to expansion, ensuring compliance with governmental requirements, and responding to the following societal trends: globalization, workforce diversity, employment at-will, flexibility in use of employees, and unions. (2) Attracting, developing, and maintaining an effective workforce first involves attracting and selecting the specific number and skills needed; second, it includes developing and training through such means as OJT, orientation, classroom, computers, conferences, and performance appraisal; and third, it involves maintaining the workforce through management of salary, benefit, and termination programs.

In your own words, *what did the above paragraph say?*   Perhaps the following will help you translate the above and strengthen your understanding of the eleventh chapter!

First Sentence: Competition, Government, and Society
The human resource department provides support for the entire organization by taking care of activities that would otherwise have to be done by managers who are involved in carrying out the basic purpose of the organization.

The human resource department supports the organization through human resource activities that help it achieve its competitive objectives. For example, if a corporation believes that it needs to become more cost competitive through reduction of labor costs, the human resource department will assist in helping to manage the downsizing process or in obtaining more productive and less costly labor inputs.

The human resource department provides support by monitoring and ensuring compliance with the federal, state, and local laws or court decisions regarding the workforce.

The human resource department supports organizational objectives by being attentive to the various societal trends related to human resources. Examples of such trends and their effects include the globalization of business and businesses, which can also impact upon the need for a diverse workforce. Societal trends may offer the opportunity for more flexibility in the use of employees through temporaries or staff leasing instead of hiring permanent employees, but the flexibility may also be limited by societal abandonment of the employment at-will doctrine and the restrictions in union contracts.

Second Sentence: Attracting, Developing, and Maintaining an Effective Workforce
The human resource department is normally responsible for attracting, developing, and maintaining an effective workforce.

Attracting and selecting the specific number and skills needed begins with forecasting and planning personnel needs. It also begins with decisions concerning job designs so as to determine what will be needed regardless of whether the needs are satisfied by outsourcing, temporaries and leased personnel, overtime, or new additions to the permanent workforce.

Employees may be attracted from internal sources, external sources, or both depending on objectives regarding EEO, employee morale, the need for new ideas, and the costs and quality of those available. Selection involves matching employer and employee needs through various means such as application, interview, and tests or assessment-center devices. Selection devices will hopefully be valid in that those who score well with the device will also tend to do well on the job, whereas those who score poorly will also do poorly on the job.

Developing and training may use means such as OJT (on-the-job training), orientation to the workplace, classroom sessions, computer-based training, and conferences. Performance appraisal often focuses on expectations for the future and how well the employee has met past expectations, whether the expectations are those of the supervisor or of a wide variety of people as in the 360-degree feedback system. However, performance appraisal discussions may facilitate employee understanding, which contributes to better performance.

Maintaining the workforce involves management of salary, benefit, and termination programs. This involves decisions as to whether the company wishes to attract and retain the very best qualified employees with salary benefit packages that are superior to others. It also involves decisions concerning how termination will be used in a fair, nondiscriminatory way that shows concern for the downsized personnel and their need to transition to other sources of income.

Key Term Identification/Application

Matching Questions

Match each statement or situation with the key term that best describes it. (Note: Some terms will not be used.)

a.	human resource management	o.	on-the-job training
b.	downsizing	p.	performance appraisal
c.	discrimination	q.	360-degree feedback
d.	affirmative action	r.	halo error
e.	matching model	s.	homogeneity
f.	human resource planning	t.	behaviorally anchored
g.	recruiting		rating scale
h.	realistic job preview	u.	performance appraisal
i	selection		interview
j.	job description	v.	compensation
k.	validity	w.	job evaluation
l.	application form	x.	point system
m.	paper-and-pencil test	y.	pay survey
n.	assessment center	z.	pay-trend line
		aa.	exit interview

_____ 1.   We must do a good job of forecasting our human resource needs including the projected matching of individuals with job vacancies.

_____ 2.   Monetary and nonmonetary payments used to reward employees.

_____ 3.   In order to increase efficiency and productivity, we have eliminated 150 jobs and three layers of management.

_____ 4.   In order to prevent surprises and quick turnover, it is important in the interview process to give applicants all pertinent and realistic information about the job that they are applying for as well as about the organization itself.

_____ 5.   Basing employment decisions such as hiring, firing, and promotion on criteria that are not job related.

_____ 6.   Because Henry has a good personality and is very cooperative with his fellow workers, his supervisor rated him very highly on all aspects of his job performance, even though there were several areas that needed improvement.

_____ 7. Even though it is sometimes disagreeable, management should conduct an interview with departing individuals to determine the reasons for their separation.

_____ 8. All the activities that are performed so as to attract, develop, and maintain an effective workforce.

_____ 9. Before we promote someone to a managerial position, we have them perform a series of simulated managerial tasks and then evaluate how well they have performed those tasks.

_____ 10. When we interview someone for a position, we should always have a written list of the duties and qualifications for the job in front of us.

_____ 11. In order to avoid potential lawsuits and to justify our compensation system, we have decided to participate in the process of determining the values of the various jobs in the organization based upon an examination of job content.

_____ 12. A very important meeting, or interview, between the supervisor and the subordinate is the formal review of the subordinate's performance.

_____ 13. All the activities or practices designed to attract qualified job applicants.

_____ 14. An important step in the selection process is having the applicant fill out a written form that includes questions concerning the applicant's education, job experience, and other relevant background characteristics.

_____ 15. A process that uses multiple raters, including self-appraisal, to evaluate the employee's performance.

_____ 16. The process of choosing the applicant with the skills, abilities, knowledge, or other attributes required in a particular job.

_____ 17. Because I know that some employees will be very defensive if I give them a low performance appraisal, I am simply going to give every employee the same rating, regardless of their individual performance.

_____ 18. In order to make certain that our organization is paying our employees fairly, we are conducting a study of what other companies in the area are paying for specific jobs and skills.

_____ 19. An employee selection approach in which the organization and the applicant attempt to match each other's needs, interests, and values.

_____ 20. A performance-rating technique that relates the employee's specific performance to a set of job-related behaviors or incidents.

Multiple-Choice Questions

Consider the following situations and, utilizing the appropriate management concepts, answer the multiple-choice questions that follow.

Situation #1

You are the general manager of STAR TV, a regional retail chain specializing in televisions, small appliances, VCRs, and stereo equipment. You are responsible for effectively staffing your store.

1.   Your company faces strong competition from several other national chains, and you already have the lowest prices in town. If you are able to establish a competitive advantage, it will come from effective human resource management, which consists of:

   a.   attracting an effective workforce.
   b.   developing the workforce.
   c.   maintaining the workforce.
   d.   all of the above.

2.   In your industry there is a high turnover of personnel due to the pay and the hours required. In order to maintain high standards of customer service and to ensure the smooth operation of the store, your forecasts of human resource needs must be accurate. These forecasts are an important part of:

   a.   human resource planning.
   b.   equal employment opportunity.
   c.   globalization.
   d.   selection.

3.   You are well-aware that all of your employment decisions must be based upon job related criteria. If your decisions are based upon non-job-related criteria such as sex, age, religion, or disability, the organization may suffer from lawsuits alleging discrimination. All of the following are equal opportunity laws that must be followed EXCEPT:

   a.   Civil Rights Act Title VII
   b.   Fair Labor Act
   c.   Americans with Disabilities Act
   d.   Equal Pay Act

4.   After we determine what skills, abilities, and knowledge levels that we need, we must make sure that our listings of the job duties and desirable qualifications are up-to-date. These listings are called:

   a.   job evaluation.
   b.   job analysis.
   c.   job description.
   d.   job specification.

5.   It is now time to utilize whatever methods or activities that are necessary to attract job applicants with the required qualifications. This process is called:

   a.   recruiting.
   b.   selection.
   c.   termination.
   d.   appraisal.

6.   It is very important to know what criteria are going to be utilized in making the selection decision and that these criteria in fact relate to success on the job. This is a concern over:

   a.   reliability.
   b.   authenticity.
   c.   empathy.
   d.   validity.

7.   Experience in recruiting and selection has also taught you that employees do not appreciate surprises and that the applicant should be given all the pertinent information about the job prior to accepting the job. This process is called:

   a.   recruiting.
   b.   realistic job preview.
   c.   selection.
   d.   orientation.

8.   The first document that you examine in determining if the applicants have met the minimal qualifications for the job, such as background, education, and work experience, is:

   a.   the job description.
   b.   the job evaluation.
   c.   the application form.
   d.   a paper-and-pencil test.

9.   You remember during this process that when you were promoted from sales associate to assistant manager, the company had you take a battery of tests, including simulation of various management tasks, to ensure that you were ready for promotion. This device used to examine internal candidates is called a(an):

    a.   paper-and-pencil test.
    b.   development center.
    c.   performance appraisal.
    d.   assessment center.

Situation #2

Because you were not really sure what you wanted to do when you graduated from college, you joined the military with the intent of giving the military three years of active duty while you made some career decisions. As a college graduate you enter the military as an officer, and part of your responsibilities are managerial.

10.   One of your fundamental obligations, and one that you do not enjoy, is the process of observing and evaluating your subordinates' performance, putting it in writing, and then providing feedback to the subordinates. This process is called:

    a.   job evaluation.
    b.   performance appraisal.
    c.   employee evaluation.
    d.   job appraisal.

11.   One of the changes that you have made in your unit in order to ensure that you are fairly evaluating the subordinates' performance is having a variety of rater inputs, including a self-rating. This process is called:

    a.   360-degree feedback.
    b.   multi-dimensional evaluation.
    c.   180-degree feedback.
    d.   a panel evaluation

12.   One of the rating errors that you are trying to avoid involves allowing the performance appraisal of one exceptional area to influence other areas of the subordinate's job performance. You are attempting to avoid the:

    a.   horn effect.
    b.   homogeneity error.
    c.   halo error.
    d.   limbo error.

13. After doing accurate performance appraisals for two years, you find yourself tiring of defensive reactions of low performers, so in one set of evaluations you give all of the subordinates the same rating regardless of performance. This is called:

    a.   horn error.
    b.   halo effect.
    c.   primacy effect.
    d.   homogeneity

14. Some of the lower ranking subordinates are complaining about their pay level. After listening for awhile, you decide to put a stop to it by asking them how much their benefits are worth. Most of the subordinates don't have a clue that it costs almost 50 percent of an employee's wages to provide them with benefits. The point is that wages, salaries, and benefits, including low-price grocery stores, holidays, and vacation are forms of:

    a.   recruiting.
    b.   compensation.
    c.   selection.
    d.   forecasting.

15. In order to actually determine the validity of the claims of the subordinates in Question 14, you have decided to conduct a study of what companies in the private sector pay for comparable types of jobs requiring similar skills. This study is called a(an):

    a.   pay survey.
    b.   point system.
    c.   propensity to pay.
    d.   pay-trend.

Skill Practice Exercises

Just-Suppose Scenarios

Scenario #1

Just suppose your cousin has a rapidly expanding house and apartment painting business. He has been operating using spot contract labor, but as he expands this is becoming too unreliable. He has hired you to handle the human resource management functions of his business.

1.   Describe and explain the role of human resource planning in this situation.

2.   Since some of your cousin's business is derived from painting schools and low-income housing, which qualify as government contracts, the painting business is required to have an affirmative action plan. Explain what this means to you.

3.   How will recruiting and selection be affected by an affirmative action plan?

Scenario #2

Just suppose that you work as a department manager in a large national retail department store chain. You are responsible for human resource management within your department.

1.   Which laws do YOU need to be aware of in terms of human resource management?

2.   How do you define discrimination, and how can you avoid it?

3.   Discuss how you will utilize job descriptions and realistic job previews in making effective selection decisions.

Scenario #3

Just-suppose that as the department manager (described in Scenario #2), one of your key responsibilities is conducting performance appraisals of the 25 full- and part-time employees that work in your department.

1.   Discuss the concept of validity as it applies to performance appraisals.

2.   Why would a BARS system be the easiest performance appraisal system to defend in court but the hardest to develop?

3.   Explain how you would use the concept of 360-degree feedback in your performance appraisal process.

Personal Learning Experience

Observation

Conducting a performance appraisal interview is an extremely sensitive and yet extraordinarily important managerial task. Poorly handled, the interview can "turn off" an already motivated employee. Handled well, the performance appraisal interview can ensure that the employee is motivated to achieve company goals.

Contact a manager of an organization with which you are familiar and ask the manager permission to allow you to sit in on and observe how the manager conducts at least one performance appraisal interview.

1.   Give a brief summary of the interview. How long did it take? Who was doing the talking?

2.   Was the interview balanced, or did the manager dwell only on performance deficiencies? Was the employee told what his or her performance was and how to correct it?

3.   Evaluate the interview. How well did the manager achieve the tasks of evaluating performance and establishing employee developmental goals for the future?

4.   If you had been the person being evaluated, how would you have reacted?

Integrated Case

The Human Resource Balance Sheet

Jane Rand, LDX TechnoSystem's CEO, decided she would attempt to develop a human resource balance sheet listing the company's human resource assets and liabilities and then try to determine the reason for the situation and what could or should be done about it. She decided that her greatest human resource assets were also her greatest liabilities.

She felt that the company had been spectacularly successful in attracting, developing, and maintaining an effective workforce. Of course, many of those attracted and retained were people whose skills were now becoming obsolete, but they were educated, intelligent, and capable people who could be trained and developed to adapt to new technologies. Promotion from within had contributed to both the positive results regarding retention and the negative results regarding need for new skills.

She felt that two of the human resource programs deserved special attention. One was the system of performance appraisal. Few employees understood it or felt that it was fair, but they realized that it was vital for promotions, pay increases, transfers to other jobs, and for many other purposes. However, they did not know what was required to get a particular rating. Neither did the supervisors who prepared the reports. The supervisor would meet with the employee at midpoint during the year to discuss how he or she was doing, but after the final appraisal was written, it was turned over to a committee that would assign ratings among all employees using a bell-shaped curve. The employee was not given any of the comments from those on the committee, only the rating.

One other human resource program that she felt needed attention was the termination program. There had been no well-thought-out systematic program for downsizing. Only recently had LDX begun to cut back on its workforce. For most of its history, especially when it had been a part of the old, massive AmCom, one of its major attractions to potential employees was that it came very close to guaranteeing lifetime employment. Most of the employees at LDX had never worked for any other company; in fact, many had worked at LDX for at least twenty years and were planning to continue to do so until they were forced to retire.

Case Questions

1.   What societal trends are being overlooked by LDX, and what should Jane do about it?

2.   Jane feels that some of her personnel assets are also her liabilities.   If she decides to implement a termination program that includes downsizing, what federal laws might be especially relevant?

3.   How could the performance appraisal program be improved not only to make it a better evaluation instrument but also to use it to support training and development?

4.   Other than making changes in performance appraisal and termination programs, is there anything else that can be done by LDX's human resources department to help the company be more competitive?

Journal Entries

Directions

The Study Guide will include a requirement that you keep a journal of your thoughts from class discussions and corresponding chapter assignments as described below.

For class discussions and each chapter covered, you will log the following journal entries:

1. A summary description of Chapter 11 class discussions.

2. A brief description of one <u>personal</u> <u>management</u> <u>activity</u> relating to class discussion in Chapter 11. This activity could include a description of how you were recruited and selected for your current job.

3. A brief description of one <u>managerial</u> <u>incident</u> you have encountered <u>at work</u> as it relates to class discussion in Chapter 11. This incident may include a brief analysis of how one federal law in human resource management affects your workplace.

4. Reflections on the interrelationship of the class discussions and the out-of-class activity and incident you have recorded in 2 and 3.

In this way, you will be reporting on and verifying to what degree what you have read in the text and experienced in the classroom matches the reality of your daily personal and business life.

Your goals will be to better understand how managers really get things done through planning, organizing, leading, and controlling resources and by interacting with the firm's outside environment.

Also, this journal will serve as a means of developing your own critical thinking ability as well as your writing skill.

1.   Summary of Class Discussion

_____

_____

_____

_____

_____

_____

_____

_____

_____

_____

_____

_____

_____

_____

2.   Personal Management Activity

Activity 1 _____

_____

_____

_____

Description 1 _____

_____

_____

_____

3.   Managerial Incident Encountered

Incident 1 _____

_____

_____

_____

Description 1 _____

_____

_____

_____

4.   Reflections on Class Discussion as Related to:

Activity 1 _____

_____

_____

_____

_____

_____

_____

_____

Incident 1 _____

_____

_____

_____

_____

_____

_____

Chapter 11 Answer Key

Matching

Question	Answer	Question	Answer
1	f	11	w
2	v	12	u
3	b	13	g
4	h	14	l
5	c	15	q
6	r	16	i
7	aa	17	s
8	a	18	y
9	n	19	e
10	j	20	t

Multiple Choice

Question	Answer	Question	Answer
1	d	9	d
2	a	10	b
3	b	11	a
4	c	12	c
5	a	13	d
6	d	14	b
7	b	15	a
8	c		

CHAPTER 12—DIVERSITY IN THE WORKPLACE

Chapter Outline	Corresponding Learning Objectives
I. Valuing Diversity • Dimensions of Diversity • Attitudes toward Diversity	L.O. 1 Explain the dimensions of employee diversity and why ethnorelativism is the appropriate attitude for today's corporations.
II. The Changing Workplace	L.O. 2 Discuss the changing workplace and the management activities required for a culturally diverse workforce.
III. Affirmative Action • Current Debates about Affirmative Action • The Glass Ceiling	L.O. 3 Explain affirmative action and why factors such as the glass ceiling have kept it from being more successful.
IV. New Responses to Cultural Diversity • Changing the Corporate Culture • Changing Structures and Policies • Diversity Awareness Training	L.O. 4 Describe how to change the corporate culture, structure, and policies and how to use diversity awareness training to meet the needs of diverse employees.
V. Defining New Relationships in Organizations • What People Want • Invisible Minorities • Balancing Family Priorities • Emotional Intimacy • Sexual Harassment	L.O. 5 Explain what people expect in organizations, including the addressing of issues such as invisible minorities and sexual harassment.
VI. Global Diversity • Selection and Training • Communication Differences	L.O. 6 Describe benefits that accrue to companies that value diversity and the cost to companies that ignore it.
VII. Benefits and Costs of Diversity • The Paradox of Diversity • Benefits of Valuing Diversity • Costs of Ignoring Diversity	

Major Concepts

(1) Primary and secondary dimensions of diversity may not be accepted in an ethnocentric environment, but other organizational environments have used workforce and sociocultural changes to facilitate employee development and job satisfaction and to achieve better customer and public relations.

(2) Diversity does not simply satisfy legal requirements but seeks to break through glass ceilings by changing corporate cultures, changing internal structures and policies, and by providing diversity training. (3) Diversity may involve costs and may require careful leadership so as to obtain positive benefits from work-oriented male and female friendships while avoiding conflict and sexual harassment.

In your own words, *what did the above paragraph say?*   Perhaps the following will help you translate the above and strengthen your understanding of the twelfth chapter!

First Sentence: Resistance versus Use of Diversity
Primary dimensions of diversity include age, gender, and race, whereas secondary dimensions include education, marital status, and income.   The term "ethnocentric" is used to refer to organizations that prefer to minimize diversity.   Such ethnocentric organizations may have a "monoculture" that excludes nontraditional employees.

Many diverse organizations have used workforce and sociocultural changes as a valuable asset to facilitate employee development and job satisfaction through a more interesting environment. They achieved better customer and public relations by using employees who can better understand and better relate to specific groups.

Second Sentence: Encouraging Acceptance of Diversity
Diversity does not simply satisfy legal requirements but seeks to break through glass ceilings by changing corporate cultures, changing internal structures and policies, and by providing diversity training. In essence, the challenge is to get all members of the organization to pursue certain workforce objectives because they want to do so not just because the law says they must do so. It is much easier to control behavior than the attitudes that underlie the behavior; if the attitude does not change, the behavior may not be significantly above minimal compliance.

Third Sentence: Costs and Risks, the Need for Leadership
Very few things provide only benefits and involve no costs or risks. Attempts to achieve diversity are not an exception.   Diversity programs may require careful leadership to implement so that the benefits will exceed the costs. Hopefully, there will be positive benefits from work-oriented male and female nonsexual friendships while avoiding conflict and sexual harassment.

Key Term Identification/Application

Matching Questions

Match each statement or situation with they key term that best describes it. (Note: Some terms will be used more than once.)

a. workforce diversity
b. ethnocentrism
c. monoculture
d. ethnorelativism
e. pluralism
f. glass ceiling
g. glass walls

h. diversity awareness training
i. invisible minorities
j. sexual harassment
k. expatriates
l. high-context culture
m. low-context culture

_____ 1. In our organization, we simply use communication to exchange facts and information.

_____ 2. The belief that one's own group or subculture is inherently better than any other group or subculture.

_____ 3. Invisible barriers to important lateral movement within the organization.

_____ 4. A form of sexual discrimination and a violation of the 1964 Civil Rights Act.

_____ 5. My sister is a Canadian citizen who lives and works in the United States.

_____ 6. Hiring people with different human qualities and who belong to various cultural groups.

_____ 7. Our organization has a corporate culture in which communication is used to enhance personal relationships.

_____ 8. Some organizations have corporate cultures that accept only one way of doing things and one set of values and beliefs.

_____ 9. People that share a social stigma that is not visibly recognizable, such as AIDS.

_____ 10. I, on the other hand, believe that groups and cultures are inherently equal.

_____ 11. Invisible barriers that prevent women and minorities from reaching key management positions.

_____ 12.   Our organization does the utmost to accommodate several subcultures, including our Chinese employees who would otherwise feel isolated and ignored.

_____ 13.   Special training that is designed to make people aware of their own prejudices and stereotypes.

_____ 14.   Jonathan told a joke to a group of workers that Joan though was inappropriate, offensive, and contributed to the creation of a hostile work environment.

_____ 15.   Many women become frustrated when they discover that once they are hired into a specific department, it is very difficult, if not impossible, to switch to another department that might help their careers.

_____ 16.   Katie is one of several women in our organization who has an eating disorder, but she is concerned about the effect on her career if she confided in someone.

_____ 17.   Our organization, and top management specifically, will only accept one way of doing things (their way) and one set of values and beliefs (their values and beliefs).

_____ 18.   It is fairly easy for women and minorities to get hired here, but almost impossible for them to be promoted beyond a certain management level.

_____ 19.   Last week our whole department went on a retreat and spent the time becoming more aware of our own prejudices and stereotypes. What an eye-opener!

_____ 20.   Our organization is very businesslike in that all communication is used to convey facts and information.

Multiple-Choice Questions

Consider the following situations and, utilizing the appropriate management concepts, answer the multiple-choice questions that follow.

Situation #1

As a member of a two-person human resource department for a small company, you are responsible for (among other things) recruiting personnel to fill vacancies in your organization.

1. Your organization believes very strongly that the most qualified person for the position should be hired regardless of race, color, religion, national origin, or culture, and your hiring practices reflect this value. Your organization practices:

    a.   glass walls
    b.   glass doors
    c.   ethnocentrism.
    d.   workforce diversity.

2. The organization has come a long way in the last twenty years. Twenty years ago your organization was one of many that accepted the values, attitudes, and beliefs of the white male worker as being the only way to behave and to view work. This was an example of:

    a.   workforce diversity.
    b.   ethnorelativism.
    c.   monoculture.
    d.   pluralism.

3. Apparently twenty years ago the prevailing belief in the organization was that the dominant white male culture and beliefs were inherently superior to any other group or culture. This situation can be characterized as:

    a.   ethnorelativism.
    b.   ethnocentrism.
    c.   ethnolasticity.
    d.   pluralism.

4.   Due to some lawsuits and some changes in top management, the organization started moving toward a more pluralistic culture by sending all employees to special training that is designed to make them aware of their values, prejudices, and stereotypes. This training is called:

      a.   diversity awareness training.
      b.   sensitivity training.
      c.   expatriation training.
      d.   est training.

5.   Now your organization believes in making accommodations for several subcultures, including employees who would otherwise feel isolated and ignored. The best term for this is:

      a.   monoculture.
      b.   pluralism.
      c.   low-context culture.
      d.   ethnocentrism.

6.   Your organization is so committed to this view that it has incorporated the value that all groups and subcultures are inherently equal in its mission statement. This position is:

      a.   ethnocentrism.
      b.   high-context culture.
      c.   ethnorelativism.
      d.   monism.

Situation #2

Maria Estaban was hired by General Dynamo, a medium-sized defense contractor. She applied for the vacancy because the organization has a reputation of providing high pay and job security.

7.   The first few months on the job went fairly well. Lately her supervisor, who is a male, has been making sexual comments around her, including jokes, and leering at her. This conduct is:

      a.   sexual harassment but legal.
      b.   not sexual harassment.
      c.   is normal, harmless, and can be expected on any job.
      d.   sexual harassment and illegal.

8. In an effort to get away from her supervisor, Maria has requested a transfer to other departments several times and has been turned down each time. Some of her fellow workers have told her not to bother requesting the transfer, because once the organization has placed a woman in a department, it is almost impossible to transfer out of it. This is an example of:

    a.   glass walls.
    b.   glass doors.
    c.   glass ceilings.
    d.   glass basements.

9. After being alerted to the transfer problem, she also discovered that the organization has never promoted women above the second level of management regardless of qualifications. This is an organizational example of a:

    a.   glass wall.
    b.   glass door.
    c.   glass ceiling.
    d.   glass basement.

10. Apparently the culture of this organization can be described as a(an):

    a.   ethnorelativistic culture.
    b.   monoculture.
    c.   high-context culture.
    d.   low-context culture.

Situation #3

After a year of experiencing the organizational culture of General Dynamo and its illegal activities, Maria quit the company and found a position with General Dynamo's prime competitor, Summitt Enterprises.

11. One of Maria's most pleasant surprises came the first day on the job when she came across this statement in the employee manual : " We at Summitt Enterprises value our diverse nature as we believe in the inherent equality of groups and subcultures." This statement reflects a(an) _____ philosophy.

    a.   enthocentrism
    b.   monoculture
    c.   blind-eye
    d.   enthnorelativism

12.   Maria has been surprised by the openness of the conversations in the cafeteria and elsewhere. At General Dynamo, all conversation entailed communicating facts and information; here at Summitt, the conversations seem to serve the purpose of enhancing personal relationships. General Dynamo is a _____, while Summitt is a _____.

     a.   low-context culture, high-context culture
     b.   high-context culture, low-context culture
     c.   plural culture, monoculture
     d.   none of the above.

13.   One of the most impressive things about the culture at Summitt is that individuals with eating or drinking disorders or other problems that are not visibly recognizable feel free to talk about their situation. At other organizations, these people would be part of the:

     a.   invisible majority.
     b.   visible majority.
     c.   invisible minority.
     d.   visible minority.

14.   Summitt seems to be committed to making significant employment accommodations to these people and other subcultures. Summitt appears to practice:

     a.   monoculturism.
     b.   ethnorelativism.
     c.   ethnocentrism.
     d.   pluralism.

15.   Summitt Enterprises seems to be especially sensitive to the needs of those people born and raised in another country who now live in this country but could feel ignored and isolated here. These people are:

     a.   republicans.
     b.   expatriates.
     c.   members of a low-context culture.
     d.   members of a high-context culture.

Skill Practice Exercises

Just-Suppose Scenarios

Scenario #1

Just suppose that you work in a small- to medium-sized privately owned company. The company is owned and operated by three brothers who are all over the age of 60 and believe in the "old style" of management.

1.   Describe how you would expect these three brothers to approach the concept of diversity.

2.   Explain the concept of monoculture in terms of how it would probably relate to this case.

Scenario #2

As the manager of a service business, you are very concerned about the staffing needs of your business. Your typical employee is young and somewhat educated, but this worker is getting harder to find because many types of businesses attempt to attract this worker.

1.   If your staffing needs can no longer be met in a traditional manner, how will you staff your business?

2.   What implications does the above have for workplace diversity?

3.   Discuss and explain the costs and the benefits of diversity awareness training.

Scenario #3

Just suppose that you are a single parent with three school-aged children, and you are searching for a quality position with a quality organization.

1.   Describe (using the terms in the text) the difference between an organization with an ethnocentric culture and one with an ethnorelativistic culture. Be specific and use examples.

2.   What difference would high-context versus low-context culture make to you? Explain.

3.   What concrete difference of effect does the organizational culture have on an individual?

Personal Learning Experience

Research

Utilizing your library or the Internet, identify and read three articles that discuss the impact of cultural diversity on the workforce of today and on the marketplace in general.

1.   Summarize the articles. Were there any approaches, other than diversity awareness training, that were utilized and appeared to be effective?

2.   If you were a member of one of the organizations that you researched, how would you react? Why?

3.   How can you utilize the information presented in this chapter?

Integrated Case

Zero-Tolerance Policy

Jane Rand, the CEO of LDX, felt that there was one undeniable major achievement of the corporation: LDX was a leader in implementing diversity.

LDX had implemented a zero-tolerance policy toward discrimination and sexual harassment that covered a wide range of groups. The policy made it clear that LDX would be intolerant of intolerance. Discrimination did not have to involve overt actions and actual words, it could involve nonverbals such as facial expressions or an unfriendly manner. Not only were victims encouraged to bring forth accusations, but anyone in the company suspecting a violation of the zero-tolerance policy was encouraged to blow the whistle—that included anonymous reports. Anyone accused of discrimination or harassment would be fired unless the person accused had irrefutable evidence to demonstrate his or her innocence. Even if proven innocent, the accused would be watched very carefully thereafter. In cases in which it was not clear who to believe (the alleged victim who was accusing or the person who was being accused), the company believed that the right thing to do was to come down on the side of the victim. In some cases, the accused would be given a second chance if he or she quickly acknowledged guilt upon being accused and promised to henceforth strongly support the policy.

Jane had smashed the "glass ceiling" by implementing promotion policies directed to bring into management those who might otherwise be excluded and to deliberately use transfers to break up any "old-boy network" that might be discovered.

To help gain acceptance of diversity, all employees were required to attend periodic diversity training. All attending the training were required to memorize and recite the benefits of diversity and the reasons for eliminating any opposition. Attendees who publicly confessed their past policy violations during the training sessions were virtually guaranteed a second chance, provided their public statements were sufficiently sincere. During one session, a cynical employee humorously compared the training to Stalinist reeducation programs that he had studied in World History classes, but the trainer conducting the session was not amused. Trainers were required to report to Jane the names of all who demonstrated a failure to embrace the ideas set forth in the sessions, so the cynic was reported. Jane called the cynic's supervisor and demanded an explanation as to why the supervisor had not done a better job of positively motivating employees regarding diversity. The supervisor was then given a deadline to report back with evidence that the cynic's attitude had improved.

Performance appraisals included a specific evaluation by supervisors of the ratee's active support of diversity. Supervisors were apprised on the extent to which their employees demonstrated support for diversity in all that they said and did both on and off the job. Performance appraisals, especially the diversity comments, were used in all decisions concerning promotion, retention, and pay increases.

Jane felt that her program was now a success. Initially, there was a period of numerous harassment and discrimination complaints against supervisors. The fired supervisors claimed that some accusers were simply getting even for failure to receive a pay increase and that others had demanded special privileges in exchange for not filing a false complaint. However, now complaints seemed to be almost nonexistent. There was no longer any hint of any opposition to diversity in any informal conversations that were monitored in restrooms and the cafeteria. Fears of humor being misunderstood resulted in less joking and more serious focus on work. Fears of being accused seemed to cut back not only on romantic interests among people of different management levels but also reduced non-romantic friendships between men and women regardless of status, thus resulting in more focus on work and in turn, greater productivity. Whenever she asked anybody whether they thought the company had a good policy regarding diversity, they would always instantly answer "Yes!" in an enthusiastic manner.

Case Questions

1.   Diversity can be a potential asset for an organization. Do you think that such is the case at LDX TechnoSystems? Why or why not?

2.   Jane feels that the decline in complaints of harassment and discrimination are evidence of the success of diversity. Do you agree? Why or why not?

3.   What might Jane do to make her diversity training more effective?

4.   Jane feels that she has smashed the glass ceiling. Do you agree? Why or why not? If she has succeeded, what are the pros and cons of her approach?

Journal Entries

Directions

The Study Guide will include a requirement that you keep a journal of your thoughts from class discussions and corresponding chapter assignments as described below.

For class discussions and each chapter covered, you will log the following journal entries:

1.   A summary description of Chapter 12 class discussions.

2.   A brief description of one <u>personal management activity</u> relating to class discussion in Chapter 12. This activity could include a brief account of your personal balancing of family priorities in order to attend college and work full-time.

3.   A brief description of one <u>managerial incident</u> you have encountered <u>at work</u> as it relates to class discussion in Chapter 12. This incident may include a brief analysis of diversity and its role in enhancing or detracting from your current work unit's productivity.

4.   Reflections on the interrelationship of the class discussions and the out-of-class activity and incident you have recorded in 2 and 3.

In this way, you will be reporting on and verifying to what degree what you have read in the text and experienced in the classroom matches the reality of your daily personal and business life.

Your goals will be to better understand how managers really get things done through planning, organizing, leading, and controlling resources and by interacting with the firm's outside environment.

Also, this journal will serve as a means of developing your own critical thinking ability as well as your writing skill.

1.   Summary of Class Discussion

_____

_____

_____

_____

_____

_____

_____

_____

_____

_____

_____

_____

_____

_____

2.   Personal Management Activity

Activity 1 _____

_____

_____

_____

Description 1 _____

_____

_____

_____

3.   Managerial Incident Encountered

Incident 1 _____

_____

_____

_____

Description 1 _____

_____

_____

_____

4.   Reflections on Class Discussion as Related to:

Activity 1 _____

_____

_____

_____

_____

_____

_____

_____

_____

Incident 1 _____

_____

_____

_____

_____

_____

_____

_____

Chapter 12 Answer Key

Matching

Question	Answer	Question	Answer
1	m	11	f
2	b	12	e
3	g	13	h
4	j	14	j
5	k	15	g
6	a	16	i
7	l	17	c
8	c	18	f
9	i	19	h
10	d	20	m

Multiple Choice

Question	Answer	Question	Answer
1	d	9	c
2	c	10	b
3	b	11	d
4	a	12	a
5	b	13	c
6	c	14	d
7	d	15	b
8	a		

CHAPTER 13—LEADERSHIP IN ORGANIZATIONS

Chapter Outline	Corresponding Learning Objectives
I. The Nature of Leadership	L.O. 1 Identify personal characteristics associated with effective leaders.
II. Leadership versus Management • Position Power • Personal Power • Empowerment	L.O. 2 Explain the five sources of power and how each causes different subordinate behavior.
III. Leadership Traits	
IV. Autocratic versus Democratic Leaders	
V. Behavioral Approaches • Ohio State Studies • Michigan Studies • The Leadership Grid	L.O. 3 Describe the leader behaviors of initiating structure and consideration and when they should be used.
VI. Contingency Approaches • Fiedler's Contingency Theory • Hersey and Blanchard's Situational Theory • Path-Goal Theory • Substitutes for Leadership	L.O. 4 Describe Hersey and Blanchard's situational theory and its application to subordinate participation. L.O. 5 Explain the path-goal model of leadership. L.O. 6 Explain how leadership fits organizational situations and how organizational characteristics can substitute for leadership behaviors.
VII. New Leadership Approaches • Transactional Leaders • Charismatic Leaders • Transformational Leaders • Interactive Leaders • Servant Leaders	L.O. 7 Describe transformational leadership and when it should be used.

Major Concepts

(1) Leaders usually have positional power and may also have personal power and ability to grant empowerment. (2) Leaders may vary in personality traits ranging from those who are autocratic in their use of authority and power to those who lead democratically by participatory approaches. (3) Behavioral approaches to leadership include the Ohio State studies (consideration and the initiating structure), the University of Michigan studies (employee and job-centered leaders), and the University of Texas/Blake and Mouton's leadership grid. (4) Four contingency approaches that tend to relate leadership styles to specific situations include Fiedler's use of three elements; Hersey and Blanchard's situational theory; path-goal theory; and the substitutes-for-leadership concept. (5) New leadership approaches that go beyond the traditional transactional approach include charismatic inspiration, transformational leaders who focus on innovation and change, interactive leaders, and servant leaders.

In your own words, *what did the above paragraph say?* Perhaps the following will help you translate the above and strengthen your understanding of the thirteenth chapter!

First Sentence: Leadership Power—Positional, Personal, and Empowerment
Leaders in a formal management position usually have positional power regardless of how much or how little personal power they may have. The positional power is suggested by the job description and is virtually the same in type and magnitude for all who hold that position; however, not all in that position will have the same personal power. Positional power involves legitimate, organizationally assigned power. That power can result in the leader's ability to bestow both financial and nonfinancial rewards. On the other hand, personal power is often a result of the leader's knowledge or personality.

Leadership through empowerment involves sharing power with those at lower levels.

Second Sentence: Traits and Autocratic versus Democratic Leaders
Leaders often vary in personality traits such as intelligence, energy, and appearance. Those who focus on leadership traits attempt to identify the traits of those who were great leaders and perhaps develop the same traits.

Leaders may range from those who are autocratic to those who are democratic. Autocratic leaders use centralized authority. They use their legitimate power and ability to positively reward or negatively coerce. Those who lead democratically use a participatory approach and gain acceptance because of their expertise and referent influence.

Third Sentence: Three Behavioral Approaches
Behavioral approaches to leadership include the Ohio State studies, which focused on consideration for employees and the initiating structure. "Consideration" involves respect for subordinates and the extent to which the leader and the led share mutual trust. The "initiating structure" pertains to

the leader's goal-oriented direction of tasks. The University of Michigan studies compared employee and job-centered leaders and found that employee-centered were more successful. Blake and Mouton at the University of Texas developed a leadership grid that built on the Ohio State University and Michigan studies and compared emphasis on work versus emphasis on people. On that grid, a "9" was high and a "1" was low. The various combinations of emphasis produced environments that have been described as team, country club, authority compliance, middle of the road, and impoverished management.

Fourth Sentence: Four Contingency Approaches

There are four contingency approaches that tend to relate leadership styles to specific situations. To make that relationship, Fiedler uses three elements: leader–member relationships—i.e., the acceptance of the leader, the clarity of the task structure, and the formalization of position power. Hersey and Blanchard's situational theory extends the Blake-Mouton leadership grid with a focus on employee task readiness: those with low readiness, such as those who need training, require different leadership than those whose readiness is higher. Path-goal theory suggests that leadership may be improved by clarifying the path to the rewards or increasing the rewards, depending on the leader's behavior and style, the situational contingency, and how rewards can be used. Although it may not be possible to totally eliminate the need for leadership, in some situations substitutes for leadership may be so strong as to substitute or neutralize the need for leadership.

Fifth Sentence: Five Other Approaches

New leadership approaches go beyond the traditional transactional approach. The transactional approach uses clarified expectations for the leader's initiatives, rewards, fairness, and consideration for employees, but such leaders may not be as dynamic and inspiring as those who are charismatic or transformational leaders. Charismatic leaders inspire through shared vision, values, and mutual trust. Transformational leaders may have charismatic qualities, but they focus on innovation and change. Interactive leaders build consensus, stress inclusiveness, encourage participation, and demonstrate a caring attitude. So-called servant leaders are lower-level employees in an organization using a bottom-up approach. The bottom-up approach does not mean that all initiatives begin at the lowest organizational levels, but it does start with worker needs and seeks to unleash their creativity in a highly empowered environment.

Key Term Identification/Application

Matching Questions

Match each statement or situation with the key term that best describes it. (Note: Some terms will not be used.)

a. leadership
b. power
c. legitimate power
d. reward power
e. coercive power
f. expert power
g. referent power
h. traits
i. autocratic leader
j. democratic leader
k. consideration
l. initiating structure

m. leadership grid
n. contingency approach
o. LPC scale
p. situational theory
q. path-goal theory
r. substitute
s. neutralizer
t. transactional leader
u. charismatic leader
v. transformational leader
w. interactive leader
x. servant leader

_____ 1.   Sometimes the leadership style is redundant or unnecessary because of the situation.

_____ 2.   Many people have the ability to influence the behavior of others.

_____ 3.   I see my role as leader as someone who not only works to achieve the organization's mission and goals but also the needs and goals of my subordinates.

_____ 4.   Jim's ability to influence others often stems from his ability to punish or even recommend punishment.

_____ 5.   Concern for people and the concern for productivity are the two important variables by which a leader's behavior can be measured.

_____ 6.   Because Yvonne is the manager and has the authority of being the manager, she is able to influence others.

_____ 7.   In today's business world, it often takes a leader with a vision, and the ability to communicate that vision, to bring about innovation and change in an organization.

_____ 8.   A dimension of leadership behavior that is concerned with the extent to which the leader is sensitive to subordinates, respects their ideas and feelings, and establishes mutual trust.

_____ 9.   Distinguishing personal characteristics such as values, intelligence, and appearance.

_____ 10.   The ability to influence others due to the ability to reward them.

_____ 11.   A situational variable that counteracts a leadership style and prevents the leader from showing certain behaviors.

_____ 12.   The ability to influence peoples' behavior towards the achievement of organizational goals.

_____ 13.   Because this person is a hero, is admired, and is respected, this person can influence the behavior of many others.

_____ 14.   Someone who has the ability to motivate subordinates to go beyond expected performance levels.

_____ 15.   A leader who relies upon referent and expert power when leading subordinates. A leader who encourages participation and delegates authority.

_____ 16.   A questionaire that is designed to identify and differentiate between relationship-oriented and task-oriented leadership styles.

_____ 17.   A leader who tends to centralize authority and utilize legitimate, reward, and coercive power.

_____ 18.   A contingency leadership approach that links the follower readiness level and the appropriate leadership style.

_____ 19.   The degree to which a type of leadership behavior is task oriented and directs subordinates workplace behavior to goal achievement.

_____ 20.   A leader who is open and inclusive, who is concerned with consensus building, and who encourages participation.

Multiple-Choice Questions

Consider the following situations and, utilizing the appropriate management concepts, answer the multiple-choice questions that follow.

Situation #1
You graduated from college three years ago and are now the distribution manager for a small regional newspaper that provides news and interest articles for the elderly.

1.   The primary goal of you and your staff this year is to increase distribution by 10%. To the extent that you have the ability to influence your staff toward the attainment of this goal, you are demonstrating:

      a.   leadership.
      b.   authority.
      c.   responsibility.
      d.   consideration.

2.   This morning you told your staff to contact all of the nursing homes in the area and place sales racks in the cafeterias and other public areas. To the extent that the staff actually does this, you are utilizing:

      a.   reward power.
      b.   coercive power.
      c.   legitimate power.
      d.   referent power.

3.   One of your policies is that the staff must submit records of their sales calls, and you spot check and follow up on about 20% of the calls. You have told them that if anybody is falsifying their powers, they will be terminated. This is an example of:

      a.   legitimate power.
      b.   coercive power.
      c.   reward power.
      d.   referent power.

4.   The president of your company is a much-admired individual. He is a very dynamic individual with whom people actually enjoy interaction. For this reason, he is very successful in motivating individuals towards the pursuit of organizational goals. This is an example of:

      a.   reward power.
      b.   legitimate power.
      c.   expert power.
      d.   referrent power.

5.   One of your staff members has a very extensive marketing background; therefore, whenever this staff member speaks about distribution strategy and tactics, everybody listens, including you! This staff member has:

    a.   empowerment.
    b.   expert power.
    c.   legitimate power.
    d.   no power because they are just a staff member.

Situation #2

As a student you have seen many different types of teachers and professors, and you have decided to use the leadership terms identified in the text to describe the different categories of teachers.

6.   One of your professors knows the material very well, and when assigning material or discussing material in class, leaves little doubt that she is the teacher. It is as if she is saying to the class "I am the teacher, and I have the correct answer, so don't argue with me." As a leader she would be labeled:

    a.   democratic.
    b.   transformational.
    c.   autocratic.
    d.   interactive.

7.   Other teachers seem to show a moderate balance between concern for people (students) and concern for "production." These teachers would be at which point on the leadership grid?

    a.   9,9
    b.   1,1
    c.   1,9
    d.   5,5

8.   According to Blake and Mouton, the point towards which all leaders should be striving is:

    a.   9,9
    b.   1,1
    c.   5,5
    d.   9,1

9.   Some people say that you have to be born a teacher in order to be a good teacher. These people would say that we should be able to identify one set of personal characteristics, such as intelligence, values, and appearance, that make for a good teacher. These people apparently believe in the:

a.   contingency approach.
b.   trait approach.
c.   path-goal approach.
d.   situational approach.

10.   Other people say that successful teachers are those who can adapt their teaching or leadership style to the type of students in the class. Students that are "immature" and not ready for autonomy need to be directed in what they do. This is an example of:

a.   situational theory.
b.   the Ohio State model.
c.   the leadership grid.
d.   the LPC scale.

Situation #3

As a student you have had many part-time or short-term jobs in a variety of different situations and have worked for a variety of different types of managers and leaders.

11.   At one time you had a boss that was such an autocratic leader, not to mention micromanager, that she made all of the decisions; although you had authority, you had no corresponding power to go along with that authority. These conditions would be considered leaadership:

a.   substitutes.
b.   contingencies.
c.   neutralizers.
d.   considerations.

12.   Another time you were picked as the assistant manager over 200 other applicants based upon your LPC score. This organization believes in:

a.   the trait approach to leadership.
b.   the behavioral approach to leadership.
c.   the situational approach to leadership.
d.   the contingency approach of Fiedler.

13.   Another boss was extremely dynamic, positive, and motivational. This person had the ability to motivate others to go way beyond their previous levels of performance or any reasonable performance expectation. This leader was a(an):

    a.   servant leader.
    b.   charismatic leader.
    c.   transactional leader.
    d.   transformational leader.

14.   You have also experienced a situation in which a new leader came into the organization with such an innovative vision for the organization, and its place in the world, that it seemed as if change was anticipated and welcomed. This type of leadership is called:

    a.   charismatic leadership.
    b.   transactional leadership.
    c.   transformational leadership.
    d.   interactive leadership.

15.   You have always considered yourself a "people person." Of all the approaches to leadership, the approach that makes the most sense to you is that which emphasizes the role of the leader as consensus builder, as one who encourages participation, and one who is known as being open and inclusive. You are seeking to become a(an):

    a.   interactive leader.
    b.   situational leader.
    c.   transformational leader.
    d.   path-goal leader.

Skill Practice Exercises

Just-Suppose Scenarios

Scenario #1

Just suppose that you have recently opened your own rapid printing service outlet. Having worked in this area as a customer service representative, you are very good technically, but you know that as the owner/manager of the business, you are also going to be responsible for leading your 20-person staff.

1.   What are your organizational goals? What does leadership mean to you in this context?

2.   Describe and explain the types of power that you possess. What is the difference between having these types of power and using them?

3.   How do you evaluate the trait theory in terms of YOURSELF being the leader and manager?

Scenario #2

Just suppose that you have always enjoyed meeting people and socializing with them. Further suppose that you also identify yourself with the marketing and sales field. After taking a few classes, you have obtained a real-estate sales-agent license.

1.   The real-estate broker in your office is very much an autocratic leader. What is your reaction to this?

2.   What would your reaction be if the leader was a democratic leader?

3.   If you were just starting your real-estate sales career, how would a situational theory leader manage/lead you? How would you feel about/react to this?

Scenario #3

Just suppose that after taking the required tests, you have been appointed as a lower-level supervisor for your state government. You are directly responsible for 20 people. There are extensive rules, regulations, and policies already in place.

1.   Given the level of rules, regulations, and policies, describe and explain the level of motivation that you expect of your staff when you walk in the door.

2.   Given the limitations of the situation, what approach to leadership makes the most sense to you? How will you lead your subordinates?

3.   Explain leadership substitutes and neutralizers within this context.

Personal Learning Experience

Application

Think of the different groups to which you currently belong. For instance, you may be a student, a member of a church, and a bowling team captain, and socialize with the same people routinely.

1.   Describe the situation. Determine the types of power that you possess in this group. Do you utilize the power that you possess?

2.   Who is the leader of your group? Describe this person. What type of leadership is this person exhibiting?

3.   What conclusion can you make from the above?

Integrated Case

The Party Animal

When Dan Steele was in college, he did not strike anyone as a potential management type. In fact, he spent so much time partying that his grades suffered and his parents decided to quit subsidizing his education. They told him to get a job and support himself. If he wanted an education, he would have to earn his own money.

He did indeed get a job. He went to work as a technician at LDX TechnoSystems. Much to his parents' pleasant surprise, his performance at LDX was quite unlike his college days. He became very serious regarding his work.   In fact, he truly liked his work, which was obvious from his enthusiasm and energy.

He felt that he could contribute even more as a manager. However, LDX would not consider promoting people into management unless they had a college degree. As a result, Dan returned to college by taking night courses. This time, he really applied himself. He could see that the concepts in his courses did indeed apply in the real world and that the classes could help him as he moved up the organizational hierarchy.   Also, his socializing skills proved to be valuable. Dan was a very outgoing, dynamic, and articulate person. He was friendly and liked to be helpful. Newer people automatically sought his advice, and the more seasoned employees turned to him to articulate their concerns and suggestions to management. People at LDX saw him as an informal leader with considerable potential.

In order to achieve his objectives, Dan severely limited his socializing and partying activities. By taking a maximum course load in the evenings and on weekends, he finally got his degree.   Soon afterwards, a supervisory position became available and Dan was selected.

People in Dan's organization found many things about him to be quite impressive. For one thing, he knew each person's job. That was a big switch from the person who was the previous supervisor: that person didn't understand the technology and the problems confronting people so he wasn't able to represent the employees effectively in dealings with other departments or with higher-level management. As a result, prior to Dan, the supervisor went along with demands from others that involved unrealistic or impossible expectations.

Another thing they liked was that Dan not only knew the job and knew the company but also got to know each person individually. He seemed to be genuinely concerned about each person. In fact, he would go out of his way to figure out how he could help people. For example, when he needed to send one of his people to Chicago on an extended business trip, he could have chosen a variety of people.   However, he sent Jan Peterson, not only because she could do what was required but also because her daughter would be graduating from a school in Chicago during the period of the trip. By sending Jan, she would thus have an LDX expense-paid trip to the graduation.
As a result of Dan's focus on employee needs, Dan's employees reciprocated by trying to figure out what they could do to be of value to him.

Case Questions

1.   Discuss how Dan used positional and personal power as a leader.

2.   What leadership traits were demonstrated by Dan? Were those traits the sole reason for his success? Why or why not?

3.   Evaluate Dan from the perspective of the Ohio State studies, the University of Michigan studies, and the Blake and Mouton managerial grid.

4.   Based on the limited information given in the case study, is Dan best described as a type of leader who is transactional, charismatic, or transformational? Explain your answer.

Journal Entries

Directions

The Study Guide will include a requirement that you keep a journal of your thoughts from class discussions and corresponding chapter assignments as described below.

For class discussions and each chapter covered, you will log the following journal entries:

1.   A summary description of Chapter 13 class discussions.

2.   A brief description of one <u>personal</u> <u>management</u> <u>activity</u> relating to class discussion in Chapter 13. This activity could include a brief description of your own leadership style and how it affects your relationship with friends.

3.   A brief description of one <u>managerial</u> <u>incident</u> you have encountered <u>at work</u> as it relates to class discussion in Chapter 13. This incident may include an analysis of how situational leadership theory, if applied, would make your work unit more productive.

4.   Reflections on the interrelationship of the class discussions and the out-of-class activity and incident you have recorded in 2 and 3.

In this way, you will be reporting on and verifying to what degree what you have read in the text and experienced in the classroom matches the reality of your daily personal and business life.

Your goals will be to better understand how managers really get things done through planning, organizing, leading, and controlling resources and by interacting with the firm's outside environment.

Also, this journal will serve as a means of developing your own critical thinking ability as well as your writing skill.

1.   Summary of Class Discussion

_____

_____

_____

_____

_____

_____

_____

_____

_____

_____

_____

_____

_____

_____

_____

_____

_____

2.   Personal Management Activity

Activity 1 _____

_____

_____

_____

Description 1 _____

_____

_____

_____

3.   Managerial Incident Encountered

Incident 1 _____

_____

_____

_____

Description 1 _____

_____

_____

_____

4.   Reflections on Class Discussion as Related to:

Activity 1 _____

_____

_____

_____

_____

_____

_____

_____

Incident 1 _____

_____

_____

_____

_____

_____

_____

_____

Chapter 13 Answer Key

Matching

Question	Answer	Question	Answer
1	r	11	s
2	b	12	a
3	x	13	g
4	e	14	u
5	m	15	j
6	c	16	o
7	v	17	i
8	k	18	p
9	h	19	l
10	d	20	w

Multiple Choice

Question	Answer	Question	Answer
1	a	9	b
2	c	10	a
3	b	11	c
4	d	12	d
5	b	13	b
6	c	14	c
7	d	15	a
8	a		

CHAPTER 14—MOTIVATION IN ORGANIZATIONS

Chapter Outline	Corresponding Learning Objectives
I. The Concept of Motivation	L.O. 1 Define motivation and explain the difference between current approaches and traditional approaches to motivation.
II. Foundations of Motivation • Traditional Approach • Human Relations Approach • Human Resource Approach • Contemporary Approaches	
III. Content Perspectives on Motivation • Hierarchy of Needs Theory • Two-Factor Theory • Acquired Needs Theory	L.O. 2 Identify and describe content theories of motivation based on employee needs.
IV. Process Perspectives on Motivation • Equity Theory • Expectancy Theory	L.O. 3 Identify and explain process theories of motivation.
V. Reinforcement Perspective on Motivation • Reinforcement Tools • Schedules of Reinforcement	L.O 4 Describe reinforcement theory and how it can be used to motivate employees.
VI. Job Design for Motivation • Job Simplification • Job Rotation • Job Enlargement • Job Enrichment • Job Characteristics Model • Empowerment and New Motivational Programs	L.O. 5 Discuss major approaches to job design and how job design influences motivation. L.O. 6 Discuss new management applications of motivation theories.

Major Concepts

(1) Over the years, the approach to motivation shifted from the traditional focus to an emphasis on human relations and human resources. (2) The three major motivational perspectives consist of "content," which examines underlying needs; "process," which explains how workers select behavioral actions to meet their needs; and "reinforcement," which notes the relationship between behavior and its consequences. (3) Motivation is also approached through the design of the job and through analysis of the job characteristics model. (4) Other motivational approaches include empowerment, pay, and scheduling.

In your own words, *what did the above paragraph say?*   Perhaps the following will help you translate the above and strengthen your understanding of the fourteenth chapter!

First Sentence: From Traditional Motivation to Human Relations and Human Resources

Over the years, the approach to motivation shifted from the traditional focus to an emphasis on human relations and human resources. The traditional approach involves economic rewards. Human relations is a means of motivating that was stressed following the Hawthorne experiments during the period between the First and Second World Wars. Human resource motivation takes into account many factors and is exemplified by McGregor's Theory X and Y, which contrasted assumptions regarding the extent to which workers have to be carefully controlled.

Second Sentence: Three Major Motivational Perspectives

The content perspective focuses on underlying needs. For example, there is Maslow's hierarchy of needs. The hierarchy, which ranges from the most basic to those that become increasingly difficult to satisfy, consists of the following: physiological, safety, belongingness, esteem, and self-actualization. Alderfer's ERG (existence, relatedness, and growth) is very similar to Maslow's hierarchy. Herzberg set forth a two-factor theory involving hygiene and motivation. The hygiene factor involves potential job dissatisfiers such as working conditions and pay whereas a motivator might involve such things as recognition, accomplishment, and growth. McClelland's acquired needs theory emphasized underlying needs such as achievement, affiliation, and power, which are acquired throughout one's lifetime.

Process perspectives explain how workers select behavioral actions to meet their needs. One such explanation is equity theory: the idea that people compare their contributions and outcomes with others and achieve fairness by changing inputs, outcomes, and perceptions or by leaving the job. Another such explanation involves "expectancy": the idea that performance depends on a worker's belief regarding his or her ability to do the job and receive the rewards.

Reinforcement perspectives deal with the relationship between behavior and its consequences. Reinforcement suggests that behavior that is positively reinforced will be repeated but that which is not reinforced will not be repeated.

Reinforcement tools include reinforcement, avoidance learning, punishment, and extinction. Positive reinforcement uses positive rewards; avoidance learning removes a negative when behavior is as desired; punishment involves negatives following undesired behavior; and extinction is the withdrawal of positive rewards when a behavior is no longer desired. Reinforcement may be continuous every time a behavior occurs or the reinforcement may be partial in that it occurs only at a fixed interval, a fixed ratio, a variable interval, or a variable ratio.

Third Sentence: Motivation through Job Design and the Job Characteristics Model

Approaches to job design include job simplification, job rotation, job enlargement (greater variety), and job enrichment. Job enrichment involves more opportunity for responsibility, recognition, and growth.

The job characteristics model consists of core job dimensions, critical psychological states, personal and work outcomes, and employee growth-need strength. Core job dimensions include: skill variety; task identity or an identifiable beginning and end; task significance to the employee; autonomy or ability to choose; and feedback concerning performance. Critical psychological states include experiencing meaningfulness of work, experiencing responsibility, and knowledge of actual results. As effective use of core job dimensions and critical psychological states results in positive personal and work outcomes, such outcomes further strengthen motivation. The concept of "employee growth-need strength" refers to the fact that people have different needs for growth and development.

Fourth Sentence: Empowerment, Pay, and Scheduling

Empowerment involves delegation of authority to subordinates. Although money is not the only motivator, it can have an impact and can be designed to provide specific incentives.   Examples include pay for performance, gain sharing, ESOPs, lump-sum bonuses, and pay for knowledge. People may be motivated not only by the pay for their work but how and when they are scheduled to do the work. For some, a flexible work schedule may be very motivating.

Key Term Identification/Application

Matching Questions

Match each statement or situation with the key term that best describes it. (Note: Some terms will not be used.)

a.	motivation	q.	reinforcement theory
b.	intrinsic reward	r.	behavior modification
c.	extrinsic reward	s.	law of effect
d.	content theories	t.	reinforcement
e.	hierarchy of needs theory	u.	schedule of reinforcement
f.	ERG theory	v.	continous reinforcement schedule
g.	frustration-regression principle	w.	partial reinforcement schedule
h.	hygiene factors	x.	job design
i.	motivators	y.	job simplification
j.	process theories	z.	job rotation
k.	equity theory	aa.	job enlargement
l.	equity	bb.	job enrichment
m.	expectancy theory	cc.	work redesign
n.	E-P expectancy	dd.	job characteristics model
o.	P-O expectancy	ee.	empowerment
p.	valence		

_____ 1.   I teach because I truly enjoy the satisfaction that it gives me.

_____ 2.   There are three categories of needs: existence, relatedness, and growth.

_____ 3.   Every time our customer service representatives receive positive feedback concerning their services from customers, they are given $10.

_____ 4.   Our employees' perception of how fairly they are treated in relation to other employees is a very important factor in their performance.

_____ 5.   We know that our jobs are somewhat boring and repetitive, so we move all of our employees to a new and different job every six months they are here.

_____ 6.   I believe that people are motivated by five different categories of needs: physiological, safety , belonging, esteem, and self-actualization, and that these needs are fulfilled in a hierarchical manner.

_____ 7.   Factors that produce job satisfaction if present but job dissatisfaction if absent are not adequate. These factors do not motivate.

_____ 8.   At our fast-food restaurant, we have designed our jobs so as to increase efficiency. Each job only has one or two tasks that the employee must perform.

_____ 9.   I believe that you can best motivate someone by establishing a relationship between a behavior and its consequences.

_____ 10. Some of our employees were very bored with their jobs, so we made their jobs broader by having them do more tasks on the same skill level so as to provide them with variety and challenge.

_____ 11. I believe one of the best ways to motivate workers is to delegate power, authority, and responsibility to them.

_____ 12. A reward given by another person.

_____ 13. Positively reinforced behavior tends to be repeated, while negatively reinforced or unreinforced behavior tends to be inhibited.

_____ 14. The arousal, direction, and persistence of behavior.

_____ 15. Those motivational theories that emphasize the needs that motivate people.

_____ 16. A schedule of reinforcement in which only some occurrences of the desired behavior are reinforced.

_____ 17. My motivation to get an A in this class depends upon how I feel about my ability to achieve the A; that if I do study and work for the A, I will achieve it; and the importance of the goal itself.

_____ 18. Any job can be analyzed in terms of its core job dimensions and then can be redesigned.

_____ 19. Every worker wants to be treated fairly, so that their perceived ratio of outputs and inputs is the same as another person's.

_____ 20. Anything that causes a given behavior to be repeated or inhibited.

Multiple-Choice Questions

Consider the following situations and, utilizing the appropriate management concepts, answer the multiple-choice questions that follow.

Situation #1

One of your life-long ambitions has been to become a mathematics teacher at one of your local high schools. You know how difficult math is for some people, and you know that you will receive a high degree of satisfaction from helping people understand the subject.

1.   According to the text, your motivation to become a teacher is based upon a(an):

    a.   extrinsic reward.
    b.   intrinsic reward.
    c.   equity.
    d.   expectancy.

2.   After graduating from college, you have finally realized your primary educational goal. It is important that you now set new goals for becoming a teacher. This future situation defines what kinds of needs?

    a.   Safety.
    b.   Belonging.
    c.   Physiological.
    d.   Self-actualization.

3.   One of the things that dismays you about your new job is the pay. Not only is the starting pay much lower than you thought it would be, but it is also lower than the starting teacher pay in some nearby states. According to Herzberg, your dismay is natural, for pay is a(an):

    a.   hygiene factor.
    b.   motivator.
    c.   intrinsic reward.
    d.   none of the above.

4.   One or two of the teachers that work with you are not motivated, even though they have been teaching for a long time and their pay is now very adequate. Herzberg would explain this by pointing to the lack of:

    a.   hygiene factors.
    b.   needs.
    c.   motivators.
    d.   extrinsic rewards.

5.   After a few years of teaching you start to notice that although you are a very motivated and hard-working teacher, there are a few teachers who have been there the same length of time as you who are making the same amount of money but are not as hard-working or motivated as you. This situation does not seem right to you. As you feel yourself becoming more demotivated as time progresses, you realize that you have compared your ratio of inputs and outputs to someone else, which is utilizing:

        a.   several content theories.
        b.   equity theory.
        c.   expectancy theory.
        d.   ERG theory.

Situation #2

It is now a few years after college, and you are married with two children. Although they are young (4 and 5 years old), you feel that they should be doing a better job of cleaning up their room and helping out by doing a few chores.

6.   The children know that they have the ability to clean up their room, and they know that if they put in the effort, the room could be spotless. The problem is that the goal of a clean room:

        a.   has a low valence.
        b.   has a high valence.
        c.   has little equity value.
        d.   has some equity value.

7.   As you think about this situation a little further, you realize that you really don't care if they want to clean up the room or not. What you really care about is the behavior itself. You also make the assumptions that positively reinforced behavior will be repeated and negatively or unreinforced behavior will be inhibited. This set of assumptions is known as:

        a.   reinforcement theory.
        b.   behavior modification.
        c.   reinforcement.
        d.   the law of effect.

8.   You also realize that the key to the situation is that positive reinforcement is:

        a.   an ice cream cone.
        b.   having you read a book to them.
        c.   words of encouragement.
        d.   anything that causes a given behavior to be repeated.

9.   Initially you have decided that every time they clean up their room to your satisfaction, they will be given a candy bar. You have chosen:

   a.   a partial reinforcement schedule.
   b.   a very dangerous reinforcer.
   c.   a continuous reinforcement schedule.
   d.   a reinforcer that will always work.

10.   As time goes on, you commence varying the reinforcement and varying the timing of the reinforcement. Now you have chosen:

   a.   a partial reinforcement schedule.
   b.   behavior modification.
   c.   a continuous reinforcement schedule.
   d.   a tactic that will not work.

Situation #3

You own and operate an office supply store. The store currently employs 25 people, both full- and part-time. Lately you have noticed that you are experiencing a very high turnover rate of personnel, and many of your employees seem to have a very apathetic attitude towards work and customer service. After realizing that screaming at them will not work, you think back to your college courses and some conversations concerning motivation.

11.   You have decided to look at the manner in which you have divided up tasks and determined jobs and then determine what effect that has on the motivation of the workers. You are approaching your problems from the viewpoint of:

   a.   behavior modification.
   b.   the process of motivation.
   c.   job design.
   d.   expectancy theory.

12.   After observing the employees and thinking about the situation, you realize that some of the problem is that, in an effort to improve task efficiency, you have reduced the number of tasks of each employee; this has resulted in boredom and turnover. Your initial approach to job design had been based upon:

   a.   job enlargement.
   b.   job simplification.
   c.   job design.
   d.   job enrichment.

13. Your next step is to analyze each job in terms of skill variety, task identity, task significance, autonomy, and feedback and then base your job redesign choices upon the findings. You are approaching your problems from the standpoint of:

a. job simplification.
b. job characteristics model.
c. job enlargement.
d. job enrichment.

14. You have determined that in order to retain the efficiency of job simplification and also deal with current levels of morale, motivation, and job satisfaction, the best tactic is to have every employee move from one job to another job every four months to provide the workers with variety. This technique is called:

a. job enrichment.
b. job enlargement.
c. job design.
d. job rotation.

15. Even though your attempt at moving employees from job to job on a periodic basis has had a moderate degree of success, you notice that after a year of doing this, you have a very well-trained—but bored—staff. You have decided to delegate much of your authority, power, and responsibility to your subordinates. This management tactic is called:

a. empowerment.
b. job enrichment.
c. positive reinforcement.
d. the ERG theory.

Skill Practice Exercises

Just-Suppose Scenarios

Scenario #1

Just suppose that it is close to graduation and you have no idea what you want to do with your life. One of your friends has suggested that you utilize your musical talents and form a band. Surprisingly enough, you are giving this half-joking suggestion some serious consideration

1.   Analyze this choice in terms of intrinsic and extrinsic rewards for yourself.

2.   Utilizing the hierarchy of needs theory, analyze which needs being a band member would satisfy and, therefore, where you would be on the hierarchy.

3.   How does the ERG theory relate to the above?

Scenario #2

Just suppose that you have always wanted the safety and security of a civil service job with the federal government. After taking several tests and waiting for a job opening for several months, you have finally landed a job in the civil service.

1.   You have always been self-motivated, but you notice that several of your co-workers are not. Analyze this from the perspective of equity theory.

2.   What do you think that you will do and why?

3.   Now analyze the same situation from the perspective of hygiene factors and motivators.

Scenario #3

Just suppose that you are the supervisor of 25 people at a large distribution warehouse. One of your problems is excessive tardiness in your department and its affect on your production level.

1.   If you were utilizing expectancy theory, how would you handle this situation? Be specific!

2.   Now you have decided to utilize reinforcement theory to deal with the tardiness issue. Discuss how you would do so.

3.   Are any job design concepts pertinent to this situation? If so, which ones?

Personal Learning Experience

Interview

Contact a local school or hospital and make an appointment to talk to one of the teachers or nurses.

1. Why is the person that you are talking to a teacher or nurse? What are the rewards of the position? What are the disadvantages of the position?

2. If they could change their job in any manner, how would they change it?

3. What does the organization that they work for do to motivate them?

4. Evaluate your interview in terms of the concepts discussed in the text. What are your conclusions?

Integrated Case

The Unmotivated Employee

Dan: "Sarah! I am Dan Steele, your new supervisor. Glad to have you aboard! Your new job here will be much different than the work you used to do in Randy's department. I imagine you have lots of questions or comments, so what is the first one?"

Sarah: "For now, I would just like to make a comment. I asked to be transferred into your organization because you have a reputation at LDX for being fair and being concerned about people's needs. Randy was a fine person and supervisor, but there were certain things about me that he could never quite understand.

"Randy seemed to value employee motivation above all else. An employee was deemed to be motivated if he or she was enthusiastic about the job and was committed to a career with LDX. That does not describe me at all.

"First of all, my job was to take packages and load them onto a truck; how can anyone become excited about that? I thought it might help to reduce monotony to not simply do the same boring job all the time, so I sometimes filled in for the person who wrapped the packages. That way I could have some variety by doing a different boring job.

"Secondly, I had never planned to spend the rest of my working life at LDX, and I do not intend to do so now. That does not mean that I am unmotivated. It is just that LDX is an interim step in a long series of steps that will get me to where I hope ultimately to be. I have a dream concerning what I hope some day to do with my interests in music. Just because LDX is only one of those steps does not mean that I am not committed to carrying out all of my responsibilities in an outstanding manner.   After all, LDX may not always need me, either. At some point as their markets and technologies change, they may not have a place for me in the company anyway. If LDX cannot assure me of lifetime employment, why should I be expected to assure LDX of my lifetime service?

"One other problem I had was that there are some music classes I would like to take that are always held during the daytime. Since Randy's department works 24 hours a day, I couldn't understand why my hours couldn't be adjusted so that I could attend the classes. However, he said that if he scheduled special hours for me, then everyone would want special hours and—since he didn't want to be accused of favoritism—the whole operation would become pure anarchy.

"In any event, maybe instead of being so honest about my feelings, I should have simply told Randy what he wanted to hear. When promotions and better jobs became available, those who professed eternal dedication to LDX got them, not me, even though (from my biased point of view) I think I was better qualified."

Case Questions

1.   How could Dan apply content theory to motivate Sarah?

2.   How would you apply process theory in understanding how to motivate Sarah?

3.   How might Randy, Sarah's former supervisor, use job design to improve motivation in his department?

4.   Note the objection of Randy to modifications in scheduling.   Do you agree? Why or why not?

Journal Entries

Directions

The Study Gguide will include a requirement that you keep a journal of your thoughts from class discussions and corresponding chapter assignments as described below.

For class discussions and each chapter covered, you will log the following journal entries:

1.   A summary description of Chapter 14 class discussions.

2.   A brief description of one <u>personal</u> <u>management</u> <u>activity</u> relating to class discussion in Chapter 14. This acitivity could include a brief description of what motivates you to carry forth with your personal growth goals.

3.   A brief description of one <u>managerial</u> <u>incident</u> you have encountered <u>at work</u> as it relates to class discussion in Chapter 14. This incident may include denoting an example of job enlargement as a tool for implementing change in your work setting.

4.   Reflections on the interrelationship of the class discussions and the out-of-class activity and incident you have recorded in 2 and 3.

In this way, you will be reporting on and verifying to what degree what you have read in the text and experienced in the classroom matches the reality of your daily personal and business life.

Your goals will be to better understand how managers really get things done through planning, organizing, leading, and controlling resources and by interacting with the firm's outside environment.

Also, this journal will serve as a means of developing your own critical thinking ability as well as your writing skill.

1.   Summary of Class Discussion

_____

_____

_____

_____

_____

_____

_____

_____

_____

_____

_____

_____

_____

_____

_____

2.   Personal Management Activity

Activity 1 _____

_____

_____

_____

Description 1 _____

_____

_____

_____

3.   Managerial Incident Encountered

Incident 1 _____

_____

_____

_____

Description 1 _____

_____

_____

_____

4.   Reflections on Class Discussion as Related to:

Activity 1 _____

_____

_____

_____

_____

_____

_____

_____

_____

Incident 1 _____

_____

_____

_____

_____

_____

_____

Chapter 14 Answer Key

Matching

Question	Answer	Question	Answer
1	b	11	ee
2	f	12	c
3	v	13	s
4	k	14	a
5	z	15	d
6	e	16	w
7	h	17	m
8	y	18	dd
9	q	19	l
10	aa	20	t

Multiple Choice

Question	Answer	Question	Answer
1	b	9	c
2	d	10	a
3	a	11	c
4	c	12	b
5	b	13	b
6	a	14	d
7	d	15	a
8	d		

CHAPTER 15—COMMUNICATING IN ORGANIZATIONS

Chapter Outline	Corresponding Learning Objectives
I. Communication and the Manager's Job • What Is Communication? • The Communication Process	**L.O. 1** Explain why communication is essential for effective management.
II. Communicating among People • Perception and Communication • Communication Channels • Nonverbal Communication • Listening	**L.O. 2** Define the basic elements of the communication process. **L.O. 3** Describe how perception, nonverbal behavior, and listening affect communication among people.
III. Organizational Communication • Formal Communication Channels • Informal Communication Channels	**L.O. 4** Describe the concept of channel richness, and explain how communication channels influence the quality of communication among managers. **L.O. 5** Explain the difference between formal and informal organizational communications and the importance of each for organization management.
IV. Communicating in Teams	**L.O. 6** Describe team communication and how structure influences communication outcomes. **L.O. 7** Discuss how open communication and dialogue can enhance team spirit and effectiveness.
V. Managing Organizational Communication • Barriers to Communication • Overcoming Communication Barriers	**L.O. 8** Describe barriers to organizational communication, and suggest ways to avoid or overcome them.

Major Concepts

(1) Managers spend a majority of their time in the communication process using various channels, verbal and nonverbal communication, and listening. (2) Team and other organizational communication involves both formal and informal communication flowing upward, downward, and horizontally. (3) Although there are individual and organizational barriers to communication, they may be overcome through individual skills and organizational actions.

In your own words, *what did the above paragraph say?* Perhaps the following will help you translate the above and strengthen your understanding of the fifteenth chapter!

First Sentence: Communication Time, Process, Verbal and Nonverbal, and Listening

Managers spend 80% of their time communicating. Communication is a process by which information is exchanged and understood by two or more people, usually to motivate or influence. The process involves encoding, sending, decoding, and feedback, if two-way communication is involved. Perception may be selective and it may require careful channel design to ensure that the decoded message is the same as that which was encoded.

Not all communication channels have the same capacity and "richness" or effectiveness. They differ regarding their ability to handle multiple cues, facilitate rapid two-way feedback, and provide a personal focus. Face-to-face communication tends to be the richest or most effective.

During face-to-face communication, not all communication is verbal or related to words. Some of the most powerful forms of communication consists of nonverbals such as variations in the voice and body language. Nonverbal messages can be conveyed also through the office surroundings. Listening is a powerful tool to use in such interactions to not only understand others but to communicate messages. (The way you listen communicates your concern about the person and what they are saying.) Listening can be an active, not just passive, form of communication.

Second Sentence: Formal and Informal; Upward, Downward, and Horizontal

Formal and informal communication flows downward, upward, and horizontally. Examples of formal downward topics include the following: goals and strategies, instructions and rationale, procedures and practices, performance feedback, and indoctrination. Examples of formal upward topics include the following: problems and exceptions, suggestions, performance reports, grievances and disputes, and financial and accounting information. Examples of formal horizontal communication includes the following: interdepartmental problem solving, coordination, and staff advice.

Examples of informal communication include "management by wandering around" and the grapevine. The grapevine becomes stronger when formal communication is ineffective or there is significant change.

Team communication can be enhanced by maintaining open communication and encouraging dialogue. Complex team communication works best if it is decentralized.

Third Sentence: Overcoming Individual and Organizational Communication Barriers

The barriers to communication are both individual and organizational. Individual barriers include interpersonal issues such as emotions and perceptions, wrong channels (writing when face-to-face is more appropriate), semantics (how words are interpreted), and inconsistent verbal and nonverbal messages. Organizational barriers include status and power differences, differences in departmental goals and needs, communication flows not fitting task needs, and the absence of formal channels for upward, downward, and horizontal communication.

Individual barriers may be overcome by developing individual skills. Those skills include listening actively, selecting the appropriate channel, making a special effort to understand others' perspective, and managing by wandering around. Organizational barriers may be overcome by developing a climate of openness and trust, using formal channels in all directions, using multiple channels, and designing a communication structure to fit specific communication needs.

Key Term Identification/Application

Matching Questions

Match each statement or situation with the key term that best describes it. (Note: Some terms will not be used.)

a.   encode
b.   message
c.   channel
d.   decode
e.   feedback
f.   perception
g.   perceptual selectivity
h.   perceptual organization
i.   stereotype
j.   channel richness
k.   nonverbal communication
l.   listening
m.   formal communication
     channel

n.   downward communication
o.   upward communication
p.   horizontal communication
q.   informal communication
     channel
r.   management by wandering
     around (MBWA)
s.   grapevine
t.   centralized network
u.   decentralized network
v.   open communication
w.   dialogue
x.   semantics
y.   communication

_____ 1.   There has been no announcement, but we are all talking about the pending downsizing.

_____ 2.   All blondes are dumb.

_____ 3.   The meaning of words and the way they are used.

_____ 4.   Last week we had a meeting of all store managers and discussed some mutual problems.

_____ 5.   I can tell from the expression on her face that she is not happy with the situation.

_____ 6.   I try to constantly and consistently be in direct contact with my workers to see how they are doing and to communicate information. I try to avoid the use of memos and other indirect methods of communication.

_____ 7.   The carrier of a communication.

_____ 8.   In our industry we need to be as creative and innovative as possible, so we break down communication barriers and actively encourage all team members to communicate directly and freely with other team members.

_____ 9. Even though we have a fairly large organization, we strongly encourage communication from lower-level workers to top management.

_____ 10. Most policy and procedural guidelines are sent from top management to lower-level employees.

_____ 11. Two days after I sent a letter to Mr. Jones, I received his response.

_____ 12. We cannot see the value in having organizational secrets, so we share all types of information throughout the company.

_____ 13. In our office I receive insurance information from two other workers, and when I am finished with it, I pass it on to another worker, who then passes it on to another.

_____ 14. The amount of information that can be transmitted during a communication episode.

_____ 15. The process by which information is exchanged and understood by two or more people.

_____ 16. The process of making sense out of one's environment.

_____ 17. Even in a crowded and noisy room, if your name is mentioned, you hear it and pay attention.

_____ 18. When an employee in accounting picks up the telephone to request information from a friend in production, it is an example of a communication channel existing outside formally authorized channels.

_____ 19. The selection of symbols with which to compose a message.

_____ 20. When a communication channel flows within the chain of command or task responsibility as defined by the organization.

Multiple-Choice Questions

Consider the following situations and, utilizing the appropriate management concepts, answer the multiple-choice questions that follow.

Situation #1

One of your friends owns a flower shop that employs 10-15 people but is experiencing a high turnover rate. Having been turned to for assistance, you observe the operation for a few days and conclude that your friend does not understand the importance and fundamentals of communication.

1.   "After telling my employees how to take care of the flowers, they either do it incorrectly, do it incompletely, or do nothing." Apparently your friend does not understand that communication is the:

    a.   sending of information.
    b.   receiving of information.
    c.   shared understanding of the information.
    d.   all of the above.

2.   Your friend explains to you that she orally gives the employees the directions for the care of the plants. Sometimes this process takes as long as 25 minutes. Apparently she is choosing the wrong:

    a.   message.
    b.   channel.
    c.   encoding.
    d.   decoding.

3.   During the process of giving directions, your friend notes that the employees only seem to be focusing on one or two key points and ignoring all the rest. This is an example of:

    a.   perceptual selectivity.
    b.   perceptual organization.
    c.   channel richness.
    d.   semantics.

4.   When asked to describe her "typical" employee, she responds, "My employees are mostly typical teenagers: young, stubborn, lazy, and ignorant." It is clear that she is suffering from:

    a.   perceptual selectivity.
    b.   perceptual organization.
    c.   forming stereotypes.
    d.   poor encoding.

5.   When you ask your friend about her nonverbals during her oral communications with her employees, she wonders why that is important. You explain that nonverbals such as her tone of voice and her facial expressions account for _____ percentage of message interpretation.

    a.   93
    b.   27
    c.   47
    d.   55

6.   Your friend believes that giving orders and directions are her major communication requirements. You spend quite a long time convincing her that today there is a new skill that she needs to work on and that is:

    a.   decoding.
    b.   channel selection.
    c.   listening.
    d.   encoding.

7.   If she develops the new skill identified in question 6 above, then she will be encouraging:

    a.   horizontal communication.
    b.   vertical communication.
    c.   formal communication.
    d.   upward communication.

8.   Another communication technique that you suggest she use would substitute for her daily direction-giving sessions; instead, she would interact directly with the employees throughout the day in order to give them information. This communication technique is known as:

    a.   MBA
    b.   BWA
    c.   MBWA
    d.   WAM

9.   One of your friend's complaints is that there seems to be a tremendous amout of misinformation being spread by word-of-mouth by the employees concerning the store, the customers, the business, and the flowers. This informal communication network is called:

    a.   the grapevine.
    b.   upward communication.
    c.   the centralized network.
    d.   the decentalized network.

Situation #2

After working for others for several years, you have decided to open your own management consulting firm. One of your fundamental assumptions is that poor communications underlies most organizational problems.

10.   One of your clients is a health insurance company that routinely processes hundreds of claims a day. Perhaps the first concern of a communication expert, such as yourself, is to install an effective:

     a.   informal communication channel.
     b.   formal communication channel.
     c.   centralized network.
     d.   decentralized network.

11.   In a relatively stable environment such as an insurance company, it makes senses to establish a structure in which team members communicate through a single individual in order to solve problems or make decisions. This structure is known as:

     a.   a decentralized network.
     b.   an informal communication channel.
     c.   MBWA.
     d.   a centralized communication network.

12.   You have also become aware of a lack of coordination of efforts and energy between departments. One department or area does not know what another area is doing, so much duplication of effort occurs. In order to correct this problem and ensure effective coordination of efforts, you establish different methods of:

     a.   downward communication.
     b.   upward communication.
     c.   horizontal communication.
     d.   open communication.

13.   Another client organization wishes to emphasize customer responsiveness. It is a small architectural firm in competition with some of the larger firms, and they believe that their competitive advantage is their size. In order to capitalize upon this, they need communication structures that are flexible. Apparently this organization is committed to participatory management and:

     a.   a centralized network.
     b.   a decentralized network.
     c.   downward communication.
     d.   semantics.

14.   In response to their request and their needs, you have suggested that information flow freely across functional barriers throughout the organization. You are advocating:

   a.   open communication.
   b.   downward communication.
   c.   a centralized network.
   d.   the perceptual organization.

15.   One of the key points that you attempt to stress and emphasize for all of your clients is that all managers and supervisors need to be aware of the importance not only of nonverbals, but also the meaning of words, and how they are used. You are emphasizing the importance of:

   a.   formal communication channels.
   b.   the grapevine.
   c.   semantics.
   d.   informal communication channels.

Skill Practice Exercises

Just-Suppose Scenarios

Scenario #1

Just suppose that you have just landed your first supervisory position in a nationwide computer retail chain. The company sells hardware and software and has established itself as a market leader due to its fast, efficient, and quality customer service.

1.   You are now preparing for your first meeting with your employees. Analyze this situation in terms of the communication process.

2.   Given that communication is the exchange and understanding of information, describe your approach to ensure that the employees understand what you are saying.

3.   Discuss the role and importance of semantics in your meeting.

Scenario #2

Just suppose that you are an English teacher for grades 6 through 8 in your school. You are well aware of the difficulties inherent in communicating with this age group and their limited attention span.

1.   Discuss the role and importance of nonverbals in this situation.

2.   Due to the nature of the job, much of the communication is downward. How can you change that?

3.   What is the value of horizontal communication for the students in this situation? How would you encourage it?

Scenario #3

Just suppose that you have entered the Navy and are preparing a research paper on communications in this organization.

1.   Describe the types of formal communication channels that you are likely to observe in this situation.

2.   Describe the communication network in existence. Is this appropriate for this situation?

3.   How important is the grapevine? As a manager, how could you utilize the grapevine to your advantage?

Personal Learning Experience

Observation

As a student you have been exposed to many different facets or elements of the college that you attend, such as the library, financial aid office, registration, student records, and classrooms. Choose one such environment and observe it from the viewpoint of communication.

1.   Describe the communication process that your observe. What channels are being used? How would you describe the channel richness? Are the channels appropriate?

2.   Identify the different types of nonverbals that you observe. What is their effect?

3.   How is feedback obtained? How effective are the listening skills of the individuals observed? Be specific!

Integrated Case

The Field Trip

Jane Rand, CEO of LDX, noticed Dan Steele walking around his department chatting with everyone and checking to see if anyone had any questions or need for help. That was not unusual for him. It used to upset her that he didn't spend more time in his office, but she could not challenge the fact that his organization seemed to lead every other department in achieving its goals. Furthermore, he seemed to be developing a reputation as a rising star, a fact that caused some in higher management to fear that he might someday take their jobs.

She told him that a college class would be touring the facility that afternoon and she wondered if he could take a moment to talk with them in the conference room. He told her that he would be glad to do so.

That afternoon, she introduced him to the class and stayed around for a few minutes to see if she could get some insight into his supervisory success by observing his communication techniques.

He started out by asking each person to introduce themselves and explain what they hoped to learn during the tour. He looked at each person very intently as each one spoke and then responded, using that person's name—often several times. He seemed relaxed, joking with people and sharing his experiences in college and on the job as the introductions continued. However, he was simultaneously repeating in his mind the names of all who had previously been introduced. As a result, when the introductions were complete, he said: "Now that you have all introduced yourselves, let me check to make sure that I have your names straight. Correct me if I mess up in any way." He then went around the room and correctly identified all twenty people present. Throughout the rest of the meeting, he would always respond to each person by name and would do so in a manner that showed a sincere interest in each person's questions or comments.

As Jane continued to observe, she thought to herself: "When I was talking to these students, they all sat there as if they were attending a funeral. Now that Dan is talking to them, they are all enthusiastic and seem to be really interested in what is going on at LDX. I wonder what is the secret of his success?"

Case Questions

1.   How did Dan communicate nonverbally?

2.   Was Dan effective primarily because of his speaking skills or his listening skills? Explain your view.

3.   How could the informal communication that Dan used in his organization have contributed to his success?

4.   Jane wondered why Dan seemed to be more effective in dealing with the students than she had been. What do you think is the answer? Explain.

Journal Entries

Directions

The Study Guide will include a requirement that you keep a journal of your thoughts from class discussions and corresponding chapter assignments as described below.

For class discussions and each chapter covered, you will log the following journal entries:

1.   A summary description of Chapter 15 class discussions.

2.   A brief description of one <u>personal</u> <u>management</u> <u>activity</u> relating to class discussion in Chapter 15. This activity could include an example of how your perception of a family member dictates how you communicate with each other.

3.   A brief description of one <u>managerial</u> <u>incident</u> you have encountered <u>at work</u> as it relates to class discussion in Chapter 15. This incident may include the role of informal conversation in your organization and how it constrains the real work from getting accomplished.

4.   Reflections on the interrelationship of the class discussions and the out-of-class activity and incident you have recorded in 2 and 3.

In this way, you will be reporting on and verifying to what degree what you have read in the text and experienced in the classroom matches the reality of your daily personal and business life.

Your goals will be to better understand how managers really get things done through planning, organizing, leading, and controlling resources and by interacting with the firm's outside environment.

Also, this journal will serve as a means of developing your own critical thinking ability as well as your writing skill.

1.   Summary of Class Discussion

_____

_____

_____

_____

_____

_____

_____

_____

_____

_____

_____

_____

_____

_____

2.   Personal Management Activity

Activity 1 _____

_____

_____

_____

Description 1 _____

_____

_____

_____

3.   Managerial Incident Encountered

Incident 1 _____

_____

_____

_____

Description 1 _____

_____

_____

_____

4.   Reflections on Class Discussion as Related to:

Activity 1 _____

_____

_____

_____

_____

_____

_____

_____

_____

Incident 1 _____

_____

_____

_____

_____

_____

_____

Chapter 15 Answer Key

Matching

Question	**Answer**	**Question**	**Answer**
1	s	11	e
2	i	12	v
3	x	13	t
4	p	14	j
5	k	15	y
6	r	16	f
7	c	17	g
8	u	18	q
9	o	19	a
10	n	20	m

Multiple Choice

Question	**Answer**	**Question**	**Answer**
1	d	9	a
2	b	10	b
3	a	11	d
4	c	12	c
5	a	13	b
6	b	14	a
7	d	15	c
8	c		

CHAPTER 16—TEAMWORK IN ORGANIZATIONS

Chapter Outline	**Corresponding Learning Objectives**

I. Teams at Work
    ● What Is a Team?
    ● Model of Work Team Effectiveness
	L.O. 1 Identify the types of teams in organizations.
	
	L.O. 2 Discuss new applications of teams to facilitate employee involvement.

II. Types of Teams
    ● Formal Teams
    ● Self-Directed Teams	

III. Work Team Characteristics
    ● Size
    ● Member Roles
	L.O. 3 Identify roles within teams and the type of role you could play to help a team be effective.

IV. Team Processes
    ● Stages of Team Development
    ● Team Cohesiveness
    ● Team Norms
	L.O. 4 Explain the general stages of team development.
	
	L.O. 5 Explain the concepts of team cohesiveness and team norms and their relationship to team performance.

V. Managing Team Conflict
    ● Causes of Conflict
    ● Styles to Handle Conflict
	L.O. 6 Understand the causes of conflict within and among teams and how to reduce conflict.

VI. Benefits and Costs of Teams
    ● Potential Benefits of Teams
    ● Potential Costs of Teams
	L.O. 7 Discuss the assets and liabilities of organizational teams.

Major Concepts

(1) Informal and formal teams, including those that are self-directed, are not simply groups but instead consist of several types of effective vertical and horizontal teams. (2) Work teams with an appropriate number of members with task and socioemotional roles will normally go through four stages during which cohesiveness and norms will be developed. (3) There are multiple causes of conflicts as well as multiple styles and techniques to handle those conflicts so that team benefits can be maximized and their costs minimized.

In your own words, *what did the above paragraph say?*   Perhaps the following will help you translate the above and strengthen your understanding of the sixteenth chapter!

First Sentence: Teams: Informal and Formal, Self-directed, Vertical and Horizontal

A team is not just a group, it consists of people who have a sense of shared mission and responsibility. Their effectiveness is based on productive output and personal satisfaction.

Formal teams are vertical and horizontal. Vertical teams may also be known as functional or command teams due to the fact that they are usually single departments involving a manager and subordinates in a hierarchy with several levels. Horizontal team members are at the same organizational level but include members with different expertise and from different departments. The two most common horizontal teams include the task force and committee. The task force is a cross-functional team that is formed for a specific activity and then disbanded when the purpose is accomplished. In contrast, the committee is permanent and deals with recurring problems. Some special-purpose teams may be withdrawn from normal involvement in the organizational structure.

Self-directed teams sometimes begin as problem-solving teams. Self-directed teams usually include people with several skills and from various functions. They are able to be self-directed because they have access to resources and are empowered with decision-making authority. They may even select their own supervisor.

Second Sentence: Numbers, Roles, Four Stages, Cohesiveness, and Norms

Work teams consist of five to twelve employees with seven often regarded as ideal. The members usually perform task or socioemotional roles, although some perform dual roles or are simply nonparticipatory. Task roles include initiating solutions, giving opinions, seeking information, summarizing, and energizing. Socioemotional roles include encouraging, harmonizing, reducing tension, following, and compromising.

Work teams may go through certain stages of development such as forming, storming. norming, performing, and adjourning. After forming, the "storming" refers to a period of conflict. "Norming" occurs after the conflict is solved and consensus is established. "Performing" involves the accomplishment of the assigned task. "Adjourning" occurs after the task has been accomplished and involves activities related to wrapping up, including any ceremonies for completion.

The level of team cohesiveness is affected by the degree of team interaction, shared goals, personal attraction to the team (do people enjoy being together?), competition with other teams, record of success, and recognition by outsiders. Outcomes resulting from cohesiveness involve morale and productivity. Generally, the more cohesive, the higher the morale. Regarding productivity, it appears to be more uniform among all team members due to pressures for conformity, but the overall productivity of the entire team is not always greater.

Team norms serve as a shared standard of conduct that guides member behavior. They tend to be informal, not written. They are affected by critical events in team's history, primacy (precedents), carryover behavior (norms brought by individual members from other environments), and explicit statements designed to initiate norms.

Third Sentence: Conflicts, Handling Conflicts, Team Benefits and Costs
Causes of conflict within teams include competition for scarce resources, jurisdictional ambiguities regarding responsibilities, communication breakdowns, personality clashes, power and status differences, and goal differences. There are several styles and techniques that may help resolve or avoid such conflicts.

Assertive/cooperative styles include competing, compromising, accommodating, and collaborating. "Competing" refers to an assertive style that may be needed for emergencies and unpopular decisions. "Compromising" is a combination assertive/cooperative style. "Accommodating" involves being cooperative. "Collaborating" is both assertive and cooperative, but this style is used to ensure that both sides win. Techniques for resolving conflicts include the use of superordinate goals (a goal that requires all to pull together), bargaining, clear definition of task responsibilities, mediation, and the facilitation of communication.

Potential benefits of teams include increased motivation, diverse knowledge and skills, satisfaction of team members, and organizational flexibility. Potential costs of teams include power realignments (loss of status and jobs), free riding (not doing one's share), and legal hassles from unions.

Key Term Identification/Application

Matching Questions

Match each statement or situation with the key term that best describes it. (Note: Some terms will not be used.)

a.	committee	n.	adjourning
b.	special-purpose team	o.	team cohesiveness
c.	problem-solving team	p.	norm
d.	self-directed team	q.	conflict
e.	virtual team	r.	team
f.	task specialist role	s.	formal team
g.	socioemotional role	t.	vertical team
h.	dual role	u.	horizontal team
i.	nonparticipator role	v.	superordinate goal
j.	forming	w.	mediation
k.	storming	x.	social facilitation
l.	norming	y.	free rider
m.	performing	z.	coordination costs

_____ 1.   I am one of seven employees in the molding department who meet to discuss different ways of improving quality, efficiency, and the work environment.

_____ 2.   Our group has been together for awhile and now our personalities and roles are starting to emerge. This is causing some conflict.

_____ 3.   Our team has split into two factions, and we have decided to bring in an independent third party to help us resolve our dispute.

_____ 4.   I have devoted a great deal of personal time and energy to our team so as to help the team reach its goal.

_____ 5.   The employees in my department all wear a suit and tie to work even though there is no written dress code.

_____ 6.   A unit of two or more people who interact and coordinate their work to accomplish a specific goal.

_____ 7.   Terry is a member of our team at school and will receive the same grade that the team does, but he has not contributed any effort or energy.

_____ 8.   Our baseball team members have a strong sense of belonging to the team, being part of the team, and wanting to remain associated with the team.

_____ 9.   When the boss steps into the room, it has a positive effect on our motivation and performance level.

_____ 10.   Our team has finally progressed to the point where it is focusing on problem solving and accomplishing the main task of the team.

_____ 11.   At our school some of our faculty are on a permanent team that regularly meets to discuss curriculum development.

_____ 12.   He isn't the best worker, but he does a good job of providing emotional support for other team members, and promoting social unity.

_____ 13.   I am part of a fifteen-member unit that is responsible for producing an entire engine and is supervised by an elected team member.

_____ 14.   She is the manager of a ten-person customer service team.

_____ 15.   Our job is done and the members of our team are preparing to disband.

_____ 16.   A goal that cannot be reached except through the joint efforts of all team members.

_____ 17.   She is an exceptional team member: not only does she provide emotional support for team members, but she is also an outstanding contributor to the work of the team .

_____ 18.   The four of us just recently got assigned to work on this project. Right now we are meeting and getting acquainted.

_____ 19.   Someone still needs to spend the time and energy that are needed to coordinate the team to enable it to perform.

_____ 20.   A team created by the organization as part of the formal organization structure.

Multiple-Choice Questions

Consider the following situations and, utilizing the appropriate management concepts, answer the multiple-choice questions that follow.

Situation #1

Your medium-sized company is in the process of negotiating a collective bargaining agreement with the union. You have been appointed as one of the team members representing management at the table.

1.   Your collective bargaining team could best be described as a(an):

   a.   committee
   b.   special-purpose team
   c.   problem-solving team
   d.   self-directed team

2.   During your initial meeting with your other team members, the team spends quite a bit of time getting acquainted with each other and somewhat oriented to the task at hand. Your team is now in the:

   a.   forming stage.
   b.   storming stage.
   c.   norming stage.
   d.   performing stage.

3.   After a few team meetings, conflict breaks out over the priorities of the team and how you are going to achieve them. The team is now in the:

   a.   adjourning stage.
   b.   norming stage.
   c.   storming stage.
   d.   performing stage.

4.   Lois is the Human Resource Director of your organization and is an excellent team member. She does a good job of providing her expertise to the collective bargaining process, and still provides emotional support for other team members during stressful negotiations. She is performing a:

   a.   task-specialist role.
   b.   socioemotional role.
   c.   participator role.
   d.   dual role.

5. The collective bargaining process is now well underway. The current contract ends December 31, and it is now December 14. Both negotiation teams are now working very diligently on hammering out a collective bargaining agreement that both sides can live with. Both teams appear to be in the:

   a. forming stage.
   b. storming stage.
   c. norming stage.
   d. performing stage.

6. All the team members seem to get some of their identity from being a team member and are attracted to the team. All team members feel that once this round of negotiations is over, they are ready to start working as a team to get ready for the next round. The team members:

   a. have a high degree of team cohesiveness.
   b. have a low degree of team cohesiveness.
   c. are in the norming stage.
   d. are in the adjourning stage.

7. The goal of negotiating a contract and performing all the work that is necessary in order to effectively do so is simply something that could not be done by a single person. This goal is called a:

   a. subordinate goal.
   b. superordinate goal.
   c. social facilitator.
   d. coordinating cost.

8. In retrospect one problem that the team encountered was that at least 15 minutes of every team meeting was spent in determining when team members were available for the next meeting. This time and energy that was needed to coordinate team activities is called:

   a. team cohesiveness.
   b. social facilitation.
   c. coordination costs.
   d. storming.

Situation #2

After extensive testing and interviewing, you have been hired as a manager in your state's Department of Revenue. You will have a staff consisting of one secretary, ten data-entry operators, and four investigators.

9.   As recognized on the organizational chart, your department reflects a:

      a.   horizontal team.
      b.   vertical team.
      c.   committee.
      d.   informal team.

10.   Your team members consistently recognize each other's birthdays, holidays, and even Fridays by alternating the duty of bringing in donuts for the department. This shared conduct is also known as a(an):

      a.   event.
      b.   social facilitation.
      c.   norm.
      d.   task-specialist role.

11.   In one of your private discussions with one of your team members, the person admitted that there was an abundance of peer pressure to maintain top performance within the department. This effect on the individual motivation and performance level by the presence of others is also known as:

      a.   social facilitation.
      b.   performing.
      c.   team cohesiveness.
      d.   none of the above.

12.   After working in this enviable position for over two years, one of the members of the team has left, and a new person has been hired. During this person's probation period, you note that he does not work nearly as hard as the rest of the department, but all other team members work even harder to make up for his lack of production. He is:

      a.   a bum.
      b.   performing a dual role.
      c.   performing a socioeconomic role.
      d.   a free rider.

13.   You have decided to terminate the person described in question #12 because he is performing a:

      a.   task-specialist role.
      b.   socioemotional role.
      c.   dual role.
      d.   nonparticipator role.

14.   After observing the smoothly functioning operation of your team, you decided to leave the day-to-day operations and decisions up to your team members; you would simply act as a third party who helps resolve conflict and disputes. You are, in essence then, acting as a(an):

   a.   investigator.
   b.   free rider.
   c.   mediator
   d.   nonparticipator

15.   Basically you see yourself as one who coordinates the activities of the team so it can perform its task. Your time, energy, and salary could be considered:

   a.   social facilitation.
   b.   coordination costs.
   c.   cost of goods sold.
   d.   none of the above.

Skill Practice Exercises

Just-Suppose Scenarios

Scenario #1

Just suppose that you are the Business Department Dean at a college and are responsible for the work of 3 secretaries and 27 faculty members. Your boss has just returned from a week-long seminar on the use of teams in education. She has directed you to prepare a report on how you will implement teams in your department. The report is due in two weeks.

1.   What is a team? Does your organization currently have any teams? Explain.

2.   Explain how you could use the team concept to complete the report requirement.

3.   What would be the advantages and disadvantage of implementing self-directed teams at this point?

Scenario #2

Just suppose that you are the Human Resource Manager for an organization that provides in-home health care. Your 50 employees are unionized and negotiations are commencing in six months.

1.   It is your job to appoint the negotiation team. What type of team is it? Identify the stages of team development that you can expect your team to undergo, with associated behaviors.

2.   Identify the roles that individual team members might assume.

3.   What do you consider your most challenging tasks as team leader?

Scenario #3

Just suppose that your organization is considering downsizing in order to remain as productive as other organizations in your industry that have already downsized.

1.   Describe the effect of downsizing on team cohesiveness.

2.   Discuss the conflict that downsizing would create and how you would handle the conflict.

Personal Learning Experience

Research

In your local library, or utilizing the Internet, research at least two articles/occurrences in which organizations have utilized teams and their experiences with teams are described.

1.   Discuss the similarities and differences among the situations.

2.   What are the advantages and disadvantages of self-directed teams?

3.   If you were a manager in one of these situations, how would you have utilized the information presented in the text on teams?

Integrated Case

Exploring Space

Jane Rand, CEO at LDX TechnoSystems, used a number of permanent committees to assist in dealing with recurring problems. One of those problems was space. Her organization provided a variety of highly technical forms of training, including hands-on training, which involved use of some very large and bulky equipment. The training was provided to people who came to her training center from various organizations around the world. There was a constant need to figure out how the limited space available could be adjusted to meet changing needs.

For years, LDX had a space committee that met each month to thrash out problems and come up with recommendations for her. A supervisor by the name of Glenna was made chairperson of that committee. It was a job that Glenna truly hated because she tended to be held responsible if the committee did not develop solutions—but what could she really do? The people who were on the committee were from all levels in the organization, and she was not in any position to force anyone to cooperate. Furthermore, very few did cooperate. Those who had a vested interest in securing space for their department's activities always seemed to believe that their need was greater than everyone else's need; therefore, it was almost impossible to get people to come to an agreement. There were some on the committee who were simply awaiting retirement. Those with a vested interest came to the meetings well-prepared and those who were coasting until retirement almost never did anything they were asked to do.

However, LDX obtained a major contract that would double its volume of training within two years. Something would be needed besides trying to get by with their current facility through such means as scheduling activities in the evenings or at customer locations. Alternatives such as computer based training would not accommodate all of their needs. Jane didn't know what to do; should she expand the facility at its current location, build a new facility at a different location and move everything to the new facility, obtain an additional facility somewhere in the local area—or was there some other solution? She decided to turn the problem over to her space committee.   She explained that once they came up with a recommendation, they would also be responsible for implementing it—so it had better be very good!

Glenna was frightened. This was a whole new mission for the committee. It would consume all of her time and leave no time for her previous duties. Furthermore, how could anything ever be accomplished with the people who were now on her space committee? She knew that when the change in mission was announced at the next meeting, those who had been previous sources of trouble would be even more dangerous when they saw an opportunity to advance their interests through the expansion.

Case Questions

1.   What type of team or organization handles space at LDX? Has it become a different type of team as a result of the new mission? Explain.

2.   Since Glenna doesn't seem to have any real control over the space committee, is it self-directed?   How should it be directed so as to be more productive?

3.   Explain whether the "storming" stage applies to the space committee prior to its new mission and how it might apply as the committee undertakes its new mission.

4.   Review the causes of team conflict and the styles/techniques used to handle the conflicts. What do you recommend be done to turn the space committee into a harmonious team?

Journal Entries

Directions

The Study Guide will include a requirement that you keep a journal of your thoughts from class discussions and corresponding chapter assignments as described below.

For class discussions and each chapter covered, you will log the following journal entries:

1.   A summary description of Chapter 16 class discussions.

2.   A brief description of one <u>personal</u> <u>management</u> <u>activity</u> relating to class discussion in Chapter 16. This activity could include your thoughts on how a team you have been a part of including family, sports, or volunteer work has or has not worked and why!

3.   A brief description of one <u>managerial</u> <u>incident</u> you have encountered <u>at work</u> as it relates to class discussion in Chapter 16. This incident may include an analysis of whether or not your work unit functions as a team and what stage of team development it is in.

4.   Reflections on the interrelationship of the class discussions and the out-of-class activity and incident you have recorded in 2 and 3.

In this way, you will be reporting on and verifying to what degree what you have read in the text and experienced in the classroom matches the reality of your daily personal and business life.

Your goals will be to better understand how managers really get things done through planning, organizing, leading, and controlling resources and by interacting with the firm's outside environment.

Also, this journal will serve as a means of developing your own critical thinking ability as well as your writing skill.

1.   Summary of Class Discussion

_____

_____

_____

_____

_____

_____

_____

_____

_____

_____

_____

_____

_____

2.   Personal Management Activity

Activity 1 _____

_____

_____

_____

Description 1 _____

_____

_____

_____

3.   Managerial Incident Encountered

Incident 1 _____

_____

_____

_____

Description 1 _____

_____

_____

_____

4.   Reflections on Class Discussion as Related to:

Activity 1 _____

_____

_____

_____

_____

_____

_____

_____

_____

Incident 1 _____

_____

_____

_____

_____

_____

_____

Chapter 16 Answer Key

Matching

Question	Answer	Question	Answer
1	c	11	a
2	k	12	g
3	w	13	d
4	f	14	t
5	p	15	n
6	r	16	v
7	y	17	h
8	o	18	j
9	x	19	z
10	m	20	s

Multiple Choice

Question	Answer	Question	Answer
1	b	9	b
2	a	10	c
3	c	11	a
4	d	12	d
5	d	13	d
6	a	14	c
7	b	15	b
8	c		

CHAPTER 17—PRODUCTIVITY THROUGH MANAGEMENT AND QUALITY CONTROL SYSTEMS

Chapter Outline	Corresponding Learning Objectives
I. The Importance of Control	L.O. 1 Define organizational control and explain why it is a key management function.
II. Strategic Planning and Quality Control • Environmental Change • Steps in the Traditional Control Process	L.O. 2 Describe how organizational control relates to strategic planning. L.O. 3 Explain the four steps in the control process.
III. Organizational Control Focus • Feedforward Control • Concurrent Control • Feedback Control • Decentralized Control	L.O. 4 Describe differences in control focus, including feedforward, concurrent, and feedback control.
IV. Total Quality Management • TQM Techniques • TQM Success Factors	L.O. 5 Describe the concept of total quality management. L.O. 6 Describe the TQM techniques of quality circle, empowerment, benchmarking, reduced cycle time, outsourcing, and continuous improvement.
V. The Budgeting Process • Top-Down or Bottom-Up Budgeting • Zero-Based Budgeting	L.O. 7 Explain the advantages of top-down versus bottom-up budgeting. L.O. 8 Describe zero-based budgeting and how it applies to organizations.
VI. Trends in Financial Control • Open-Book Management • Economic Value-Added Systems • Activity-Based Costing (ABC)	L.O. 9 Describe new trends in financial control and their impact on organizations.
VII. Signs of Inadequate Budget Control Systems	L.O. 10 Describe the trends in effective organizational control

Major Concepts

(1) Organizational control is a process involving four steps that may have to be occasionally adapted to changes. (2) Three common types of control—feedforward, concurrent, and feedback—may be decentralized. (3) TQM exemplifies a decentralized, organizationwide dedication to quality that uses quality circles, empowerment, benchmarking, reduced cycle time, outsourcing, and continuous improvement. (4) Financial controls include the use of top-down, bottom-up, and zero-based budgets and recent trends such as open-book management, economic value-added systems, and activity-based costing.

In your own words, *what did the above paragraph say?*   Perhaps the following will help you translate the above and strengthen your understanding of the seventeenth chapter!

First Sentence: Four-Step Process, Adapting to Change
Organizational control is a process to bring activities into line with expectations in plans, targets, and standards of performance. Implementation of controls involves four steps: establishing standards of performance; measuring actual performance; comparing performance to standards; and taking corrective action. Internal controls must adapt to strategic changes and must not continue measuring what was important in the past but not at present.

Second Sentence: Feedforward, Concurrent, and Feedback May Be Decentralized
Most organizations use feedforward, concurrent, and feedback controls simultaneously but may place emphasis on only one or two. Feedforward control focuses on human, material, and financial resources flowing into the organization. It is also called preliminary or preventative quality control. Concurrent control involves the monitoring of ongoing employee activities to ensure consistency with established standards. Feedback control monitors outputs. Feedback is output/postaction control.

Decentralized control uses social values, traditions, common beliefs, and trust to generate compliance with organizational controls. It may be accomplished through the corporate culture, peer groups, self-control, employee selection, and socialization.

Third Sentence: TQM, an Organizationwide Commitment
Total quality management (TQM) is a philosophy of organizationwide commitment to continuous improvement, focusing on teamwork, customer satisfaction, and lowering costs. TQM focuses on decentralized control. TQM techniques include the following: quality circles, empowerment, benchmarking, reduced cycle time, outsourcing, and continuous improvement.

Quality circles (QC) are groups of 6 to 12 volunteer employees who meet regularly to discuss and solve problems that effect their common work activities. Benchmarking is the continuous process of measuring products, services, and practices against the toughest competitors or those companies recognized as industry leaders. Reduced cycle time is achieved through changes in the steps taken to complete a company process. Outsourcing involves the farming out of a company's in-house operation to a vendor.

Continuous improvement is a concept that calls for the implementation of small, incremental improvements in all areas of the organization on an ongoing basis.

Fourth Sentence: Financial Controls, Budgets, and Recent Trends

Budgeting is part of planning, but the budgeted outlays can then be compared to actual outlays for control purposes. Financial controls are thus affected by the budgeting process: top-down or bottom-up budgeting and zero-based budgeting.

Under top-down budgeting, middle and lower-level managers set departmental budget targets in accordance with overall company revenues and expenditures as specified by top management. Bottom-up budgeting involves lower-level managers budgeting their departments' resource needs and passing them up to top management for approval. Zero-based budgeting requires responsibility centers to calculate resource needs based on the coming year's priorities rather than on the previous year's activities.

Trends in financial controls include open-book management, economic value-added systems, and activity-based costing. Open-book management makes financial information and results available to all employees. Economic value-added systems measure each job, department, or process by the value added. Activity-based costing identifies the various activities needed to produce a product or service, determines the cost of those activities, and allocates financial resources according to the "true" cost of each product or service.

Be alert to indicators suggesting needs for revisions and improvements in budget-control systems.

Key Term Identification/Application

Matching Questions

Match each statement or situation with the key term that best describes it. (Note: Some terms will be used more than once.)

a.	organizational control		j.	outsourcing
b.	environmental discontinuity		k.	cycle time
c.	feedforward control		l.	continuous improvement
d.	concurrent control		m.	top-down budgeting
e.	feedback control		n.	bottom-up budgeting
f.	decentralized control		o.	zero-based budgeting
g.	total quality management		p.	open-book management
h.	quality circle		q.	economic value-added system
i.	benchmarking		r.	activity-based costing

_____ 1.   Our budgeting system involves top management specifying overall company revenues and expenses, and middle and lower-level managers then setting departmental budgets.

_____ 2.   A large and significant change in the organization's environment in a short period of time.

_____ 3.   Monitoring ongoing actions to ensure that they comply with and are consistent with standards.

_____ 4.   We think it is important to share financial information and results with all employees.

_____ 5.   The identification of the various activities necessary to produce a product and the determination of the true cost of those activities, followed by the allocation of financial resources to those activities.

_____ 6.   All of the systematic processes through which management regulates organizational activities to make them consistent with plans, targets, and standards of performance.

_____ 7.   The use of social values, traditions, common beliefs, and trust to ensure compliance with organizational goals.

_____ 8.   A small group of six to twelve employees who meet voluntarily to discuss and solve problems that affect their workplace.

_____ 9.   The identification and measurement of all the activities the company does to add value to a product.

_____ 10.   The steps taken to complete a company process.

_____ 11.   A control system that focuses on the human, material, and financial inputs flowing into the organization.

_____ 12.   The continuous process of measuring company products, services, and practices against that of the toughest competition or industry leaders.

_____ 13.   Budgeting based upon the calculation of financial resource needs based on the coming year's priorities rather than on last year's budget.

_____ 14.   A control system that focuses on the organization's outputs.

_____ 15.   The farming-out of an organization's in-house operations.

_____ 16.   Our entire organization is committed to continuous product and process improvement. We focus on teamwork, customer satisfaction, and lowering costs.

_____ 17.   In our organization the lower-level managers initiate the budgetary process by budgeting their departments' resource needs and passing them up to top management for approval.

_____ 18.   We believe in making a large number of small and incremental improvements throughout the organization on an ongoing basis.

_____ 19.   In order to be hired, you must meet a certain level of skill and aptitude requirements. After you are hired, you must participate in an extensive program. All this happens before you begin working on the product.

_____ 20.   I farm out the marketing and accounting functions to other companies and simply concentrate on my business, which is cleaning carpets.

Multiple-Choice Questions

Consider the following situations and, utilizing the appropriate management concepts, answer the multiple-choice questions that follow.

Situation #1

As the owner of a small-town grocery store, you are well aware of the encroachment of the large national grocery chains. You feel that the only competitive advantage that you can claim is your friendly customer service.

1. You have decided to focus your energy on producing the friendly customer service that you seek. In your hiring process you look for a "people" person, and you also define the expectations that you have in terms of providing the friendly customer service. You are focusing your energies on:

    a.   feedforward control.
    b.   concurrent control.
    c.   feedback control.
    d.   decentralized control.

2. You have also decided to employ the services of a "secret shopper" in an effort to better monitor employees as they provide customer service. Here you are concentrating on:

    a. feedforward control.
    b. concurrent control.
    c. feedback control.
    d. decentralized control.

3. You remember from your management days that an alternative to formally establishing many rules, procedures, and standards for your control systems is to depend on the employees' values and beliefs, trusting that they will provide the necessary level of customer service. This is called:

    a.   feedback control.
    b.   organizational control.
    c.   concurrent control.
    d.   decentralized control.

4.   During the year you are in a constant state of shock as six strong grocery competitors move into your small town and commence operations. You didn't think that amount of building and stocking was possible in such a short time frame. The organization is experiencing:

   a.   culture shock.
   b.   centralized control.
   c.   environmental discontinuity.
   d.   decentralized control.

5.   One of the management techniques that you have decided to utilize in face of this stiff competition is to compare your products, services, and practices with that of the competition in an effort to identify those practices and then improve your systems. This comparison is known as:

   a.   benchmarking.
   b.   hijacking.
   c.   total quality management.
   d.   outsourcing.

6.   You are going to utilize the benchmark process in an attempt to continuously implement a large number of incremental improvements in all areas of operation. This process is called:

   a.   total quality management.
   b.   continuous improvement.
   c.   incremental management.
   d.   continuous management.

7.   You have also decided to streamline your organization by farming out functions such as payroll and marketing to reduce your overhead expenses, cut costs, and become more productive. This process is called:

   a.   outbacking.
   b.   outsiding.
   c.   outsourcing.
   d.   total quality management.

8.   Due to the trust that you have established with your decentralized control techniques, several of your cashiers and baggers have been voluntarily meeting to discuss and solve problems in their work area. This is known as:

   a.   quality outsourcing.
   b.   quality insourcing.
   c.   a quality box.
   d.   a quality circle.

Situation #2

One of your relatives, who owns and operates a large department store, is preparing to retire and has asked if you are interested in taking over the operation. After considerable thought, you have decided to go into the department store business.

9.   The primary business philosophy that you bring with you is the insistence on providing a quality product for your customers and that quality is an organization-wide concern. You are also going to focus on teamwork, providing customer satisfaction, and lowering costs. These are the basics of:

   a.   mechanistic control.
   b.   total quality management (TQM)
   c.   outsourcing.
   d.   networking.

10.   You quickly realize that the department store business operates on a relatively narrow profit margin, which makes accurate forecasting and budgeting of primary importance. The method that the store has utilized for years is having top management (with their access to full and complete information) do the forecasting of revenues and expenses and have the various departments target their budgets in compliance with those of top management. This approach is known as:

   a.   top-down budgeting.
   b.   down-top budgeting.
   c.   bottom-up budgeting.
   d.   zero-based budgeting.

11.   Another approach that you are considering is having each department calculate their own resource needs for the coming year depending upon their priorities rather than on last year's budget.   This is known as:

   a.   top-down budgeting.
   b.   bottom-up budgeting.
   c.   open-book management.
   d.   zero-based budgeting.

12.   Another possibility is to have the lower-level managers budget their departments' resources and then pass them up to top-level management for approval. This approach is called:

   a.   reverse top-down budgeting.
   b.   zero-based budgeting.
   c.   bottom-up budgeting.
   d.   backwards budgeting.

13.   You are determined that whichever budgeting process is settled upon will have as its main cornerstone the unlimited sharing of financial information and results with all employees. This philosophy is at the center of:

    a.   benchmarking.
    b.   open-book management.
    c.   closed-book management.
    d.   by-the-book management.

14.   In addition to the importance of an effective budgetary process, you also are insistent upon establishing goals in a variety of areas. One of the key areas, of course, is sales. You have established a good control system that automatically compares this year's results with last year's results. Any control system that focuses upon the organization's outputs is known as:

    a.   an open-book control system.
    b.   delayed control system.
    c.   concurrent control system.
    d.   feedback control system.

15.   In an effort to keep tight control over the finances of the business, you have adopted a control system that identifies the various activities that are needed to produce a product or service. The system then determines the cost of that activity and allocates resources based upon the cost of the activity. This is a short description of a(an):

    a.   activity-based costing.
    b.   economic value-added system.
    c.   open-book management system.
    d.   top-down budgetary system.

Skill Practice Exercises

Just-Suppose Scenarios

Scenario #1

Just suppose that you are the new manager of a floundering restaurant. The owner has given you six months to turn the business around—or else! Your initial operational assessment is that the business lacks effective control systems.

1.   Identify an organization goal. Develop specific control systems in support of that goal in each of the following three areas:

Feedforward Control

Concurrent Control

Feedback Control

2.   Explain the appropriateness of a decentralized control system in this situation.

Scenario #2

Just suppose that you operate a small photography business that employs about 20 people and specializes in providing the customer with quality photography services in a timely manner.

1.   How could you apply total quality management (TQM) to your business?

2.   Explain how you would make use of the following:

Benchmarking

Continuous Improvement

Scenario #3

Just suppose that you are the owner of a small plastic-wrap manufacturing firm. Your year end is approaching in three months.

1.   Your previous and current approach to budgeting has been top-down. Explain this concept.

2.   What are the advantages and disadvantages of each of the following:

        Bottom-Up Budgeting

        Zero-Based Budgeting

3.   What are the benefits of open-book management?

Personal Learning Experience

Application

Many students and educators alike question the validity of grades as a true measure of learning. Assume that you are the professor of a management class and have decided to develop a new and innovative way of measuring performance and learning in the classroom.

1.   What are your goals for the course?

2.   How would you develop standards for those goals? Do so.

3.   How will you measure performance?

4.   Describe how you will compare performance to the standard.

5.   What are your choices or alternatives for corrective action?

6.   Evaluate your control system.

7.   How could you utilize these concepts in feedforward, concurrent, and feedback control systems?

Integrated Case

Controlling Controls

LDX TechnoSystems had frequently developed plans and strategies that seemed to offer a bright future. The company sought to organize its resources effectively to carry out the plans. However, there sometimes seemed to be problems regarding the controls needed to ensure that the plans were successfully implemented.

Performance standards were very high at LDX. In fact, to the extent that the standards were followed, they tended to result in a higher quality product than really interested the customer and certainly a more expensive product than was desired by much of the market. Of course, standards were often regarded as objectives that were intended to cause people to reach. However, for many of those who looked at those standards, attainment of standards was something that seemed out of their reach. As a result, a major question for many employees was simply this: what is the real standard? The one officially set forth or the one that will be accepted—and what exactly will be accepted?

Inevitably, when the standards were not met, all managers (including those who were in specialized staff positions with no connection to the product) would be brought together for lectures dealing with the need for continuous improvement. The discussion was always focused on how to bring performance up to the standard, not on whether the standard needed a downward adjustment. After all, LDX was determined to not benchmark its products and activities based on other companies; instead, it was determined to be the benchmark that all others use.

There was one area of control where the company seemed to be doing fairly well. LDX used bottom-up budgeting in which all the managers worked together to develop a budget that was submitted to Jane for approval. She assumed that it must be working because LDX's actual outlays were always within the budgeted outlays.

Case Questions

1.   Regardless of whether LDX has a formal TQM program, does its emphasis on quality and continuous improvement indicate that it is carrying out the spirit of TQM? Explain.

2.   How should LDX establish standards?

3.   Discuss the LDX attitude concerning benchmarking.

4.   Jane considers LDX's success in staying within its budget to be a sign of success. Critique
        her view.

Journal Entries

Directions

The Study Guide will include a requirement that you keep a journal of your thoughts from class discussions and corresponding chapter assignments as described below.

For class discussions and each chapter covered, you will log the following journal entries:

1. A summary description of Chapter 17 class discussions.

2. A brief description of one <u>personal</u> <u>management</u> <u>activity</u> relating to class discussion in Chapter 17. This activity chould include a review by yourself of how one of the control focus mechanisms covered in the text has helped or could help you in your daily activities.

3. A brief description of one <u>managerial</u> <u>incident</u> you have encountered <u>at work</u> as it relates to class discussion in Chapter 17. This incident can include a brief description how any one of the TQM techniques reviewed has been implemented in your work environment.

4. Reflections on the interrelationship of the class discussions and the out-of-class activity and incident you have recorded in 2 and 3.

In this way, you will be reporting on and verifying to what degree what you have read in the text and experienced in the classroom matches the reality of your daily personal and business life.

Your goals will be to better understand how managers really get things done through planning, organizing, leading, and controlling resources and by interacting with the firm's outside environment.

Also, this journal will serve as a means of developing your own critical thinking ability as well as your writing skill.

1.   Summary of Class Discussion

_____

_____

_____

_____

_____

_____

_____

_____

_____

_____

_____

_____

_____

2.   Personal Management Activity

Activity 1 _____

_____

_____

_____

Description 1 _____

_____

_____

_____

3.   Managerial Incident Encountered

Incident 1 _____

_____

_____

_____

Description 1 _____

_____

_____

_____

4.   Reflections on Class Discussion as Related to:

Activity 1 _____

_____

_____

_____

_____

_____

_____

_____

Incident 1 _____

_____

_____

_____

_____

_____

Chapter 17 Answer Key

Matching

Question	Answer	Question	Answer
1	m	11	c
2	b	12	i
3	d	13	o
4	p	14	e
5	r	15	j
6	a	16	g
7	f	17	n
8	h	18	l
9	q	19	c
10	k	20	j

Multiple Choice

Question	Answer	Question	Answer
1	a	9	b
2	b	10	a
3	d	11	d
4	c	12	c
5	a	13	b
6	b	14	d
7	c	15	a
8	d		